Ypres to V

A Collection of Photographs of the
War areas in France & Flanders

Alex. B. W. Kennedy

Alpha Editions

This edition published in 2024

ISBN : 9789362990099

Design and Setting By
Alpha Editions
www.alphaedis.com
Email - info@alphaedis.com

As per information held with us this book is in Public Domain. This book is a reproduction of an important historical work. Alpha Editions uses the best technology to reproduce historical work in the same manner it was first published to preserve its original nature. Any marks or number seen are left intentionally to preserve its true form.

Contents

PREFACE ....- 1 -
I.—INTRODUCTORY ....- 3 -
II.-THE YPRES SALIENT ....- 8 -
III.—ZEEBRUGGE ....- 31 -
IV.—THE LYS SALIENT ....- 36 -
V.—BETHUNE, LA BASSÉE, AND LOOS ....- 52 -
VI.—ARRAS, VIMY, AND LENS ....- 63 -
VII.—THE SOMME ....- 74 -
VIII.—ALBERT AND THE ANCRE ....- 99 -
IX.—THE OISE AND THE AVRE ....- 105 -
X.—CAMBRAI TO ST. QUENTIN ....- 115 -
XI.—RHEIMS, THE AISNE, SOISSONS ....- 127 -
XII.—VERDUN, THE MEUSE, AND THE ARGONNE .....- 136 -
XIII—THE MARNE TO MONS ....- 154 -
FOOTNOTES: ....- 176 -

PREFACE

AN official visit to the Front during the great days of October, 1918, when our chief difficulty and our great object was to keep up with the retreating Germans, gave me some first-hand knowledge of the devastation of the country which had been the result of four years of war. Familiar—too familiar—as this was to our soldiers, we at home—if I may take myself as a fair example of the average man—could really form no idea, even from the most vivid of the correspondents' descriptions, of what the ruined country was actually like. Roads, fields, orchards, were a featureless waste of shell-holes, often already covered with rank herbage altogether disguising their original nature. Villages were only recognisable by painted notices, "This is Givenchy," or sometimes "This *was* Givenchy"; not a house, not a wall, not a gate-post to show where they had been. Large towns like Ypres or Lens or Albert were little more than piles of brick, stone, and timber rubbish, through which roads were being cleared between immense piles of débris. In Rheims nearly as many houses were destroyed as the 13,000 said to have been burnt in the Great Fire of London, and smaller places like Soissons or Cambrai or Arras had suffered terribly. It was forbidden in our Army Areas at that time, no doubt for excellent reasons, to use a camera, but I made up my mind that when permission could be obtained I would do my best to secure some permanent record of what had happened.

It was only in September of 1919 that I was able, with my friend, Lieutenant-Colonel Douglas Gill, D.S.O., R.A., to make a first photographic visit to the War Areas, and to get over a hundred views from Ypres to Verdun. At this time Major-General P. G. Grant was in charge of affairs at Headquarters at Wimereux. It was not without pardonable professional pride that I remembered that it was General Grant, a Royal Engineer Officer, who had on the 25th-26th of March, 1918, been chosen to organise the wonderfully constituted Company which General Haig's despatch euphemistically called, in enumerating the elements of which it consisted, a "mixed force." The days were critical, the French reserves had far to come and had not reached us, and the "mixed force," brought together in a few hours, proved sufficient addition to enable us to hold on, until the enemy, exhausted, could get no farther. General Grant was kind enough to give a brother Engineer every help, especially through his Area Commanders, Colonel Falcon, Colonel Carey, and Colonel Russell Brown, to all of whom we were much indebted. The result of this visit, and a second a few months later, has been that I have been able to take nearly 250 negatives of the places which were so much in our news and in our minds during the terrible four years of the war. I have thought that it might be interesting, both to the soldiers who fought for us all over France and Flanders and to their friends at home who heard from day to day of the places where they were fighting, to have something which would show what these places were really like, to turn the too familiar names into recognisable pictures, and this is my reason for publishing these photographs. In 1919 very little had as yet been done by way of reconstruction. In the spring of 1920, happily, a great deal had been done. But the photographs which follow indicate really—as well as the imperfections of a photograph allow—the condition of the places and of the country previous to reconstruction, and I am glad to be able to show my countrymen something of the condition to which our neighbour's country was brought by the war. Some realisation of this may enable us to understand better how keenly and over poweringly the French desire that the terms of Peace with our common enemies should be such as will definitely prevent for ever the recurrence of these horrors.

In addition to my own photographs I have to acknowledge, with many thanks, permission from Sir Martin Conway to use Plates 43, 64, 68, and 73, which were taken officially at a time when outsiders were not allowed to photograph. I have also to thank Mr. Basil Mott for the use of his two picturesque views (Plates 49 and 69) of Lens and Albert under snow, Colonel Douglas Gill for the view on Kemmel Hill (Plate 32), and Mr. R. Godai for the photograph (Plate 18) of a destroyed pillbox.

ALEXANDER B. W. KENNEDY.

ALBANY,
August, 1921.

I.—INTRODUCTORY

(PLATES 1 TO 4.)

ON the 26th of July, 1914, on my return from a pleasant motor excursion through the Dolomites, I arrived at Innsbruck, and found the picturesquely situated old city in a state of unsuppressed excitement owing to the proclamation of war made on that day between Austria and Serbia. The crowds in the Maria Theresien Strasse were reading and discussing the proclamation (Plate 1), and were obviously in excellent spirits, with no premonition of what would be the unhappy fate of their country when at length the fire which they had kindled should be finally extinguished. Among the mountains we had seen no newspapers for weeks, so that the news of the outbreak of war came as a complete surprise, but still as something not at all affecting ourselves. It was not until some days later (on the 30th of July) that we found ourselves in the thick of German mobilisation at the Kehl bridge, and were told that we must find our way home either by Belgium or by Switzerland, for all roads into France were closed. After some exciting days, and many interviews with high German authorities, civil, military and police, we happily succeeded in getting safely into Switzerland, and so eventually back to England by way of Genoa, Gibraltar, and the Bay of Biscay.

The École Militaire at Montreuil (Plate 2), a sufficiently uninteresting building in appearance, is notable for us as constituting, after the removal from St. Omer in March, 1916, the offices of our G.H.Q. in France. Here the schemes were prepared, and from here the orders were issued, which—after so long a time of suspense and anxiety—resulted finally in the Allied victory of 1918. It is interesting, and perhaps not uninstructive, to compare the account of the manner of life at Montreuil, as described by the author of "G.H.Q. (Montreuil)," with that which prevailed at the German headquarters in Charleville, of which Mr. Domelier (an eyewitness throughout the occupation) gives very interesting, if sometimes scandalous, particulars.[1]

Life at Montreuil is described as "serious enough ... monkish in its denial of some pleasures, rigid in discipline, exacting in work.... Like a college where everyone was a 'swotter.'" The precautions for safety taken at Charleville differed as much from ours as its manner of life. We hear of cellars reinforced with concrete in walls and roof, of bombproof casemates with several exits and underground passages, of netted elastic buffer mattresses overhead to intercept bombs, of felted door joints to keep out gas. And yet the two places were about the same distance from the enemy's lines and were equally exposed to the enemy's air raids. The differences seem to be due to the same difference in mentality as that which showed itself in so many other matters.

And farther north the King—and the Queen—of the Belgians "occupied a little villa within range of the German guns, and in a district incessantly attacked by the enemy's bombing aeroplanes."[2]

It was at 3.30 a.m. on the 21st of March, 1918, that the great German attack westwards over the old Somme battlefields commenced. The events of the four following days—the days of the greatest anxiety to most of us since the commencement of the war—are remembered only too well and too painfully. Our armies, unavoidably thinned and for days out of reach of reserves, were, with the French beside them, continuously driven back, until the Germans were close to Villers Bretonneux (ten miles from Amiens), had crossed the Avre to the south, and had taken Albert and crossed the Ancre on the north, wiping out in a few days all our gains of 1917. At least one benefit, the greatest of all possible benefits, resulted from the extreme urgency of the situation. On the 26th of March a special conference was held at Doullens, which in 1914 had been General Foch's H.Q. The Hôtel de Ville of that town (Plate 3), otherwise a commonplace and uninteresting building—in which the conference met—became at once a building notable for ever in history. Lord Milner and General Sir Henry Wilson, who were fortunately in France, attended, with President Poincaré, M. Clemenceau, and M. Loucheur, as well as Sir Douglas Haig, with our four Army Commanders, and General Pétain and General Foch. As an immediate result, arrived at unanimously by the conference,[3] General Foch was made *de facto*—and a few days later *de jure*—Generalissimo of the Allied Armies in France. It was immediately after this decision (on the 28th of March) that General Pershing nobly offered to General Foch, for serving under his authority in any way which he thought most useful, every man whom he had available of the Americans who had arrived. From the moment when, under such conditions, unity of command was at length achieved, and in spite of the further set-backs in Flanders in April—Ludendorff's last despairing efforts—the ultimate issue of the war was no longer in doubt.

Just within the forest of Compiègne, about four miles from the town, is a certain little knot of railway tracks (Plate 4), close to the main Compiègne-Soissons road, on which took place, on the 8th of November, 1918, surely the most memorable conference since 1870. There were present General Foch and his Chief of Staff, General Weygand, Admiral Sir Rosslyn Wemyss, and Admiral Sims in their saloon on the rails to the left, the German representatives being brought up on the farther track and crossing over to General Foch's carriage. An account of the interview which has been published states that Herr Erzberger said in the first instance that he had come to receive proposals for an armistice, and that General Foch refused altogether to discuss matters on any such basis, and until Erzberger had admitted that he had come "to beg for an armistice."[4] The now well-known terms by which an armistice would be granted, on conditions equivalent to absolute surrender, were then given to the Germans under the obligation of their acceptance within three days. With their final acceptance hostilities ended at 11 o'clock on the forenoon of the 11th of November.

PLATE I.

THE DECLARATION OF WAR.

The principal street in Innsbruck, the capital of Southern Austria, on the 30th of July, 1914, when crowds were reading the Declaration of War between Austria and Serbia.

PLATE II.

G.H.Q.

The École Militaire at Montreuil, which was used as the offices of our G.H.Q. during the greater part of the war.

PLATE III.

DOULLENS.

The Hôtel de Ville at Doullens, where, on the 26th of March, 1918, General Foch was appointed as de facto Generalissimo of the Allied Armies in France.

PLATE IV.

THE ARMISTICE.

The sidings in the Forest of Compiègne where General Foch and Sir Rosslyn Wemyss, on behalf of the Allies, met Herr Erzberger and his colleagues on the 8th of November, 1918, and dictated to them the terms on which an armistice would be granted.

II.-THE YPRES SALIENT

(PLATES 5 TO 18.)

THE Ypres Salient was fought over during practically the whole of the war. The first battle of Ypres, during the "race to the sea," was in October-November, 1914, when the Kaiser stayed at Thielt (twenty-five miles north-east of Ypres) for five days at the beginning of November to be ready to enter the city, only to suffer one of his many disappointments when the "old Contemptibles" kept him out. The Germans, however, got as far as Hooge, only two and a half miles away from the city, and were there for more than two years. An extremely interesting account, which is very pleasant reading, of the close co-operation of the British and French Armies in this first Ypres battle is given by General Dubois in a book just published.[5] It was presumably when French and Foch met on the 31st of October, the most critical day, that the reported conversation occurred (if it ever occurred), in which French's view that there was nothing left but to die was met by Foch with the characteristic rejoinder that they had better stand fast first—they could die afterwards.

The second battle of Ypres lasted from April to June, 1915, and during this battle the first use of poison gas was made, at St. Julien. Except in the St. Julien region the lines remained practically where they were after the three months' fighting. In spite of this a captured order issued to the German Army in August, 1915, said that "peace in October is certain"!

Mr. Buchan tells a story characteristic of our Tommies, that during a retirement ordered in May one man "solemnly cleaned and swept out his dugout before going."[6] But this was equalled by the tidiness of the old body in Ypres (mentioned in Sister Marguerite's Journal), who came out and swept away the débris of the last shell which had burst in front of her house, quite regardless of the continuous bombardment.

The third battle of Ypres began with our capture of the Messines Ridge on the 7th of June, 1917, and lasted till November of the same year, by which time Ypres was so far "cleared" that our lines were close to Gheluvelt (five miles from the city), and extended from Passchendaele and Houthulst on the north to Messines and Hollebeke on the south.

Then in April, 1918, came the great German break-through, when the Allies lost Armentières and Bailleul, Kemmel and Messines, and the enemy was in Merville and Estaires, and was inside Zillebeke and Hooge, and less than a couple of miles from Ypres along the Menin Road.

But the city itself still and always held out.

Finally our turn came. The Merville area was retaken in August, 1918 (the 8th of August was Ludendorff's "black day"), while on the memorable day on which we crossed the Hindenburg Line on the St. Quentin Canal (28th to 29th of September) the Germans were driven for the first time back past Gheluvelt by the Belgians, the French, and ourselves, and two days afterwards they were in full retreat.

The official despatches and many war books have told about the salient, about the terrible hardships and the brave doings of our soldiers there, and those of our Allies who were with us. But they do not, because they cannot, tell us what was going on within the walls of the city itself, during those first months of the siege, while the unfortunate inhabitants were still trying to live there, hoping—one supposes—from each day to the next that the bombardment would finally come to an end. Something, however, we know of this from the account of men who were there, either as soldiers or in the Red Cross service, on equally dangerous duty. But among the civilians who were neither one nor the other the names especially of two out of many will always live in the war history of Ypres, remembered for their devotion and heroism—Sister Marguerite and Father Charles Delaere. Father Delaere was the Curé of Ypres in 1914, later on he became Doyen, and not long ago a letter from him told me that he had been made a Canon. Sister Marguerite is a native of Ypres, and was, as a nun, attached to the Convent of St. Marie, engaged largely in teaching at the outbreak of the war. Her simple duties were suddenly changed; she became not only nurse and even doctor, but carpenter, fireman, baker, barber, shoemaker—all trades! Above all, she was the universal friend and helper of the poor creatures who were incapable of helping themselves, for whom she found shelter while herself without any, and whose children she mothered when their parents lay buried under the ruins of their homes, or dying in whatever buildings served at the time for a hospital.

The Journal[7] kept by Sister Marguerite, and published in 1918 by her permission for Red Cross benefit, gives a picture of life—or existence—in Ypres during the first eight months of its siege. It is so vivid, and at the same time so simply told, that (as I fear that copies of the Journal may no longer be obtainable) I make no apology for quoting from it. It is the poignant story of war as it appeared to a woman suddenly called out of a life of peaceful work to face its realities in their grimmest form, to do so without the excitement of fighting and without the comradeship of the regiment, or even the use of the soldierly mask of humour, to cover up the unrecordable reality.

The Germans actually entered Ypres on the 7th of October, the first day on which any shells fell on the town, and one civilian was killed in his own room. But the children on that day amused themselves afterwards by picking up the shrapnel bullets! After the Germans were turned out a week later, one of their companies was found to have left behind a characteristic notice: "Les Allemands craignent Dieu et hors Lui nulle chose au monde." They had succeeded in doing a fair amount of pillaging, as well as making heavy requisitions, during their few days of occupation.

It is pleasant to find that Sister Marguerite has nowhere anything but praise for the behaviour of the British soldiers who occupied the city for so long. She tells of British wounded coming into Ypres, and with them a German wounded prisoner. A woman ran up to offer milk to the men, but, with the recollection that her husband had been killed by a German shell, would not give any to the German. A soldier, however, who had been wounded by this particular German, drank only half his milk, and passed the rest on to his prisoner. She adds: "Ce n'est pas la première fois que nous pouvons admirer pareils actes de générosité."

On the 6th of November an operation was being carried on involving the amputation of a man's hand; the Sister who had tried to act as nurse had fainted, and Sister Marguerite (herself not long out of the surgeon's hands) took her place:

"Nous commençâmes donc: la main de M. Notevaert était démise; quand, vers 2 h. ½, un obus tomba sur notre couvent et détruisit deux classes à 10 métres de l'École menagère ou nous étions. Les éclats de verre et les pierres arrivèrent jusqu'a nous et un grand trou fut fait dans le mur. Le docteur venait de faire la dernière entaille; nous étions là tous les deux, pâles de frayeur, comme dans un nuage de fumée et blancs de poussière, lui tenant encore dans sa main le bistouri et moi la main démise dans la mienne. Quelques instants nous restâmes indécis. Les blessés criaient, et en un moment tout fut sens dessus-dessous. 'Ta, ta, ta,' dit M. le docteur, 'ce n'est rien. Continuons notre besogne, car nous n'avons pas de temps à perdre.' ..."

Among the wounded at this time were three Germans, of whom one (a Prussian) refused either to eat or drink, alleging that he would be poisoned!—presumably an idea encouraged by his officers to prevent surrender. Eventually he took what the sisters gave him.

A few days later came a real baptism of fire:

"Vers 11 heures, M. le Curé me dit d'aller chercher rue du Canon deux vieilles femmes.... Comme on bombardait justement ce quartier, je le priai de me laisser attendre le moment d'une accalmie. 'Allez-y tout de suite,' me repondit-il, 'on pourrait oublier ces pauvres gens plus tard et leur vie en dépend peut-être.' 'Au nom de Dieu,' me dis-je, et je partis. Mais à peine avais-je fait quelques pas dans la rue que ... 'sss ... sss ... pon!' La tête d'un shrapnel roula dans la rue, tout près de moi. Je retournai en courant. Mais M. le Curé avait entendu le son de ma voix et de la cuisine il me cria: 'Eh bien! n'êtes vous pas encore parti?' A trois reprises je retournai pour revenir presque aussi vite. Enfins je m'enhardis et je revins cette fois avec les petites vieilles, que je conduisis au couvent. Pas moins de cinq shrapnels passèrent au-dessus de nos têtes, et vous pouvez penser si le cœur me battait.... Cependant c'est à partir de ce jour que je devins plus courageuse pour affronter les bombardements."

The "Menin Gate" of Ypres (Plate 5) is nothing now but a broad gap in the old fortifications, where the long, straight road from Menin through Gheluvelt bends round to enter the city. During the whole of the siege of Ypres—that is, in fact, during the whole of the war—this spot was continuously exposed to German shell-fire, one of the "hottest" points over the whole war area. On the left of the "Gate" Canada has purchased a certain amount of ground for a Canadian memorial. The old walls, however, have remained, and the "casemates" (Plate 6) on their inner sides were for many weeks or even months the sole refuge of the poorer inhabitants who possessed no cellars of their own. The story of how these poor folk had to be removed, perforce, both for safety and for sanitary reasons, is best told in Sister Marguerite's words:

5 *Decr.*—"Chaque famille y choisit son petit coin, y installe deux ou trois matelas, deux ou trois chaises, une petite lampe, parfois une petite table et un réchaud à pétrole. La lourde porte d'entrée[8] était entr'ouverte. Il n'est pas étonnant des lors qu'après peu de temps, des maladies contagieuses s'y déclarèrent. Des habitants restèrent six semaines dans ce réduit sans voir la lumière du jour. J'y trouvai un jour un enfant de deux mois qui y était né et n'avait pas encore respiré l'air pur du dehors."

7 *Jan.*—"Ma mission principale est de servir de guide et d'interprète et aussi de décider les malades à se laisser conduire à l'hôpital, ce qui n'était pas toujours facile! Quand les malades y consentent, l'opposition de la famille soulève de nouveaux obstacles et les protestations injurieuses souvent ne manquent pas, ces pauvres gens ne comprenant pas qu'on ne veut que leur faire du bien. Une fois même, une vieille femme empoigna la pelle à charbon et le tisonnier pour me frapper. Heureusement les messieurs anglais, ignorant la langue flamande, ne comprennent pas les termes délicats par lesquels on paye leur dévouement."

The city was left entirely in ruins (Plate 7 is a view from the wall at the South Gate), not a single building standing with walls and roof, or in any condition that could be called habitable. The ruined tower (Plate 8), of which the foundation dates from 1201, is all that remains of the once beautiful Cloth Hall, and the Cathedral of St. Martin behind it is just as completely destroyed. It is to be hoped that after the celebrations of July, 1920, the miserable restaurants with their flaunting advertisements, which seemed to smother the tragic ruins with their commonplace banalities in 1919, may be done away with. It cannot be impossible to find means by which the natural interest of visitors, for too many of whom the salient is the grave of friends and relatives, can be gratified without vulgarising ground which for generations to come will be sacred in memory to the Allies whose soldiers fought there, and whose sons it was who formed the "thin red line" which was for so long the chief barrier to hold back the German hordes from the north of France, and, in effect, from our own country.

It must be remembered, in looking at such views as Plates [7] and [8], that the clear spaces in the foreground are only clear because all the buildings upon them have been destroyed, wiped out. Before the war these spaces were closely built upon, covered all over with houses. In [Plate 7] are seen two or three "reconstructions" started after the ground had been cleared of the mass of brick and stone rubbish with which it was thickly covered until the end of the fighting. It is hardly necessary to say that the general tidiness of the ground in the Grande Place ([Plate 8]) belongs to a time months after the Germans had been driven finally out of range. During the war there was neither time nor opportunity to clear away the débris, which covered road and building sites alike.

The Ypres Salient, as we came to know it, is essentially the ground north and south of the twelve miles of road running from Ypres to Menin. Ypres itself is about 65 feet above sea-level, and Menin (on the Lys) about 35 feet. But the ground between them rises to over 200 feet at "Clapham Junction" (three miles from Ypres) and remains approximately at the same level for the two miles farther to Gheluvelt. This higher ground circles round to the south-west (through Hill 60) until it joins Wytschaete (eight miles south of Ypres) and the Messines Ridge. To the north it continues from Gheluvelt by Broodseinde, between Becelaere and Zonnebeke, to the Passchendaele Ridge (180 feet), some seven miles north-east of Ypres. The unfortunate city was therefore not only at the centre of a very narrow salient, but one in which it was encircled by higher ground on three sides within easy observation and shelling range. For a long time, until our advance in 1917, the German lines were only distant two and a half miles north, east, and south from the city, and everywhere were on levels sufficiently above that of the city to keep it always under observation.

It would have been cold comfort to our poor fellows who had to face the horrors of the Flanders mud to know that three centuries ago a traveller wrote: "Near Ypres they found the road often indistinguishable from the fields, and the mud came up to their horses' girths."[9]

But in fact the physical difficulties due to the nature of the soil, churned up by shells on every square yard, were so horrible that Lord Haig (who is certainly not given to exaggeration in his despatches) says of the 1917 advance:[10]

"Our men advanced every time with absolute confidence in their power to overcome the enemy, even though they had sometimes to struggle through mud up to their waists to reach him. So long as they could reach him they did overcome him, but physical exhaustion placed narrow limits on the depth to which each advance could be pushed, and compelled long pauses between the advances.... Time after time the practically beaten enemy was enabled to reorganise and relieve his men and to bring up reinforcements behind the sea of mud which constituted his main protection."

The statement made that "nine-tenths of the time our men were fighting Nature, and the remainder fighting Germans," cannot be much exaggerated.

It is, of course, impossible in photographs taken long after fighting has ceased, and, indeed, in any photographs except those taken from aeroplanes,[11] to give an adequate idea of what the surface of the salient was during the war. Plate 9 gives some idea of the ground beside the road, near Hooge, *after a dry summer*,[12] and Plate 10 gives a similar view, after rain, near Gheluvelt. The bit of "Tank Cemetery" at "Stirling Castle" (Plate 11) on the high ground close to "Clapham Junction," and the illustrations of Hill 60, serve also to give some rough idea, but only a very imperfect one, of the conditions. Even now one has to walk in serpentine fashion along the ridges between the shell-holes in order to make any progress. But in the war winters each shell-hole was filled with liquid, sticky mud, and over such ground our men had to advance time and again, oftener by night than by day, slithering down the slimy banks into slimier mud, scrambling up the other side somehow or other, carrying full kit all the time, and continuously exposed to murderous shell-fire from commanding positions. There can have been no condition in the whole campaign which brought out better the indomitable pluck and spirit of our infantry.

Plate 12 is taken at the cross-roads ("Clapham Junction") between "Dumbarton Wood" and "Stirling Castle" on one side and "Glen Corse Wood" on the other. It is at the highest point of the slope which falls down through Hooge to Ypres. Of the woods which our men named so picturesquely nothing whatever remains—in fact, the skeleton avenue on the Becelaere Road (Plate 13) contained more trees than were to be seen anywhere else in the neighbourhood, and even these I found to have been cut down later on. Their only use would be as firewood.

On my last visit to the salient, a year ago, reconstruction in the shape of what may be called hutments, or something a little more substantial, had commenced at the eastern end and extended as far as Gheluwe, while even up to Gheluvelt there were beginnings of attempts at cultivation. If one had not seen elsewhere what has actually been done, it would seem physically impossible that soil so utterly destroyed could be brought again into cultivation for a generation. But the Belgian and French peasants are capable of wonders.

"Hill 60" (Plates 14 and 15) is to all appearance little more than a heap of spoil from the cutting for the railway running south-eastwards from Ypres to Lille. But it forms an observation ridge some 150 feet above the level of Ypres and only two and a half miles distant from the city. It was captured by the Germans early in the war, and in April, 1915, retaken by the British after very heavy fighting, in which 3,000 bodies were said to have been left on its slopes. A month later, however, it was lost again under heavy gas attacks, and remained in German possession substantially until the great attack on the Messines Ridge in June, 1917 (the third battle of Ypres), when we once more regained it, after ten months of underground fighting and tunnelling. It was lost again during the German attack in April, 1918, and only finally recovered in the final advance in September. Long before the end this historical hummock had been riddled below ground by mines, and above ground torn up by their explosions and by incessant shell-fire, so that it is now merely a mass of craters and shell-holes, with the remains of dugouts in the soft clay.

The two illustrations give some idea of the state of the ground and a suggestion of the wide horizon commanded by this insignificant elevation.

It was on the 22nd of April, 1915, that the Germans startled and horrified the world by the use of "poison gas" at St. Julien (about three miles northeast of Ypres), making a "scrap of paper" of Hague agreements, as of everything else. Before the end of the war they must have bitterly regretted their action, but on the first appearance of the yellow death-bearing cloud it answered its purpose only too well—the Turcos were not to be blamed for flying incontinently before this devilish terror. The Allies, naturally, had no means of defence—even the wet handkerchief was not thought of, but somehow or other a couple of Canadian brigades held on magnificently—fighting poison gas unprotected must have required even more pluck than facing machine-guns—and for a time appear to have been all that stood between Ypres and the enemy. Under the date of the 22nd of April Sister Marguerite writes in her Journal:

"... Au retour de nos visites aux malades, vers 5 heures, des soldats français [Turcos] fuyant les tranchées, nous rencontrèrent, criant et hurlant que les Boches les avaient empoisonnés! Beaucoup moururent sur la route; d'autres en prie à l'asphyxie demandaient à grands cris un peu de lait. Je revins à la maison tandis que le docteur, obligé de continuer, retourna porter ses soins à une femme. Mais celle-ci, effrayée par le bombardement, s'était enfuie dans les champs où le docteur Fox la retrouva après une heure de recherches. Au couvent je trouvai d'autre soldats encore, victimes des gaz empoisonnés; on leur servait du lait chaud condensé."

"37 nouveaux empoisonnés dans la matinée du 23. Impossible de les mener plus loin que l'hôpital civil où ils sont logés dans les caves.... Nous aussi, nous reçûmes notre part: un sur le couvent, et deux, trois, aux alentours. Voilà qui est terrible! L'eau me coula des yeux, mes lèvres bleuirent, j'étais prête à suffoquer."

But the brave lady never suggests for a moment that she should leave the place, and did in fact remain in the city until the military insisted on everyone leaving on the 9th of May, when there seems to have been imminent fear of the Germans reaching the city, and when, at any rate, the Kaiser was again waiting at Thielt in expectation of entering it.

St. Julien was taken at the time, and the German line advanced to the canal some miles in front of it; but the ruined village was afterwards recaptured and gas drenched by us—a strange Nemesis—in July, 1917, and remained in our hands until the German advance in 1918. Plate 16 certainly does not suggest the tragedy which we must always connect with the name of St. Julien; it is a screen at the entrance to a Chinese camp which stood there in 1919. It illustrates, oddly enough, an ancient Chinese superstition that "spirits"—and of course spirits are always malevolent—can only go straight forward, so that if any kind of screen is placed in front of the house entrance the spirit will be unable to get in, not, apparently, having the sense to go round the barrier. The gentleman standing in front of the screen (which is in effect a huge triptych) gave us to understand that he was the artist, but our knowledge of Chinese and his of English were too limited to be very certain. The screen was certainly quite a satisfactory piece of decoration.

In 1917 we were preparing for the long-drawn attack which eventually gave us the Passchendaele Ridge (Plate 17), fighting for months over such ground as the foreground of the photograph shows. Defence by such means as the construction of a "Hindenburg Line" was quite impossible in the mud and slime of the salient, and Von Armin devised the scheme of what we came to call "pillboxes." Each pillbox was a structure (Plate 18) of reinforced concrete, often large enough to hold thirty or forty men with machine-guns, and strong enough to give protection from everything short of a direct hit by a large shell. They were only raised above ground-level sufficiently to allow the guns to be worked, their entrances being, of course, at the back. They were echeloned along behind the front line, and connected and protected by barbed-wire entanglements. They proved a serious difficulty when we first had to deal with them in July-August, 1917. General Haig says:

"Many were reduced as our troops advanced, but others held out during the day, and delayed the arrival of our supports."[13]

But a few months later General Plumer had devised tactics which countered the pillboxes very successfully, and eventually the German machine-gunners found that it was better to come out and fight in the open, and even to surrender, rather than be cooped up and grenaded when our men got round to the entrance. Already in October captured documents showed that the German High Command were inclined to prefer their old methods to the new ones.[14]

The fight to reach the Passchendaele Ridge (the distant rising ground shown in Plate 17) lasted in effect from July to November of 1917. The Germans fought hard and well, but our chief enemy, as always in the salient, was the weather, and its effect in covering the whole ground with muddy slime.

The much-coveted Passchendaele Ridge is only about 120 feet higher than the level of Ypres; it is the continuation northwards of the rising ground which crosses the Menin Road at Gheluvelt and passes through Becelaere and Broodseinde. But, once attained, it affords a clear view over the flat Belgian country towards Roulers for many miles, just as in the hands of the enemy it afforded a clear view over Zonnebeke and St. Julien to Ypres.

The fight for the ridge was a long, tedious, and costly affair of many months, and although we gained it, and incidentally gained the knowledge of how to circumvent the pillboxes, the delays which had been caused by the weather conditions prevented us from attaining the full advantages that had been—quite reasonably—hoped for and expected.

PLATE V.

THE MENIN GATE OF YPRES.

This gap in the old walls of Ypres is the entrance of the road from Menin, which runs for some eleven miles straight across the middle of the Salient by Hooge, Gheluvelt and Gheluwe, known throughout the war as the "Menin Road."

PLATE VI.

DUGOUTS IN THE WALLS OF YPRES.

The Casemates and Dugouts on the inner side of the old fortifications of Ypres were the refuge of hundreds of the inhabitants of Ypres—especially those who had no cellars of their own—in 1914-15.

PLATE VII.

YPRES FROM THE LILLE GATE.

This view is taken from the City Wall above the South or Lille Gate of the City. The church of which some white ruins are seen is St. Pierre. The whole of the bare ground in the foreground was once covered closely with buildings, but of these hardly a trace remains. Some beginnings of reconstruction are already to be seen.

PLATE VIII.

THE BELFRY TOWER AT YPRES.

The Belfry Tower of the beautiful Cloth Hall of Ypres was the oldest part of the building. The upper part of the tower itself has gone entirely, and of course also the beautiful spire. The foundation of the Tower was laid in 1201.

The Cathedral of St. Martin, of which a few ruins are seen, stood behind and to the west of the Cloth Hall. It is entirely in ruins.

PLATE IX.

THE "TANK CEMETERY," HOOGE.

In the Salient south of the Menin Road, at Hooge, about three miles from Ypres. With so much water lying after a hot summer, it can be imagined what the shell-holes were like after continuous rain. The country was hopeless for tanks, and horrible beyond description for our poor fellows who had to fight in it.

PLATE X.

GHELUVELT.

The Village of Gheluvelt, on the Menin Road in the Salient, no longer exists. But some parts of it stood on and round about this wet piece of ground.

PLATE XI.

"STIRLING CASTLE."

Why this little shell-holed hummock received its name is unknown. It is on the south side of the Menin Road between Gheluvelt and Hooge, and is obviously a portion of the "Tank Cemetery."

PLATE XII.
"CLAPHAM JUNCTION."

At the cross-roads on the highest point of the Menin Road, some 130 feet higher than Ypres itself. The half-derelict Tank was one of the many such wrecks which strewed the Salient.

PLATE XIII.

THE ROAD TO BECELAERE.

Most of the Road Avenues in the Salient east of Ypres have disappeared entirely, by shell-fire and poison gas in the first instance, and then by cutting down. This particular Avenue, a branch from the Menin Road, still remained at the end of the war showing at least what it might once have been. The dead trunks have now been cut down.

PLATE XIV.
"HILL 60."

Many elevations in Flanders and France are known by their heights, in metres, over sea-level. On so flat a country the importance of "Hill 60," and many another such point, as a position for observation, is of course out of all proportion to its absolute height. This Hill, so bitterly fought over, is only some 60 or 70 feet higher than the surrounding country.

PLATE XV.

"HILL 60."

What is left of a mine crater on "Hill 60," with a suggestion of the wide horizon over the Salient obtained from this horrible heap of churned-up clay.

PLATE XVI.

ST. JULIEN.

On the site of the German first gas attack, on the 22nd of April, 1915, stood in 1919 a large camp of Chinese, employed in clearing and levelling the shell-struck ground and preparing it to some extent for agricultural operations. The painted screen guarded the entrance to the camp.

PLATE XVII.

THE PASSCHENDAELE RIDGE.

A photograph taken in the north of the Salient with the long low line of the Passchendaele Ridge in the distance. It gives some idea of the way in which the whole land surface is covered with weeds and shell-pits.

PLATE XVIII.

A "PILLBOX."

The wreck of one of the German Pillboxes, of very heavily reinforced concrete, such as were brought into use with some flourish of trumpets in July, 1917, but very successfully countered by General Plumer's methods later on.

III.—ZEEBRUGGE

(PLATES 19 TO 23.)

THERE would be no object in recapitulating here the story of the attack on Zeebrugge on St. George's Day of 1918. Every schoolboy for generations will, it is to be hoped, know it by heart.

Plate 19 shows the magnificent proportions of the canal which covers the eight miles from Bruges to Zeebrugge. It was used continuously during the war for the passage of submarines from their enormous concrete shelters at Bruges—which had resisted all the attacks of our bombers—to the sea. Bruges, in fact, is really the port; there is no port at Zeebrugge except a small dock and the open water under the shelter of the great curved mole. The gates of the lock at the seaward end of the canal are huge caissons (Plate 20) which slide into place from recesses on the western side of the lock, one of which can be seen in the photograph, in which the seaward gate is shown in its closed position. Between the two gates the lock is crossed by a girder bridge which can be swung to one side in the usual way to allow the passage of vessels. It is a matter of history that the lock gates of 1798 were blown up by a British naval party, but our bombers had not been successful in hitting the gates of 1915, so that they were intact at the time of our attack, and remained so till the end. By way of preparation for any possibilities, however, the Germans had got a spare caisson standing beside the canal ready to be put in place if either of the others should be destroyed.

It will be remembered that the great curved mole at Zeebrugge is a mile long, and about 175 feet in breadth over much of its length, carrying several lines of railway and huge warehouses. Many of the latter are at present destroyed, and a postcard purchased on the spot gives an illustration of some of these, with the quaint superscription: "Magazins des Allemands incendiés par les Tommies pour détruire les innombrables puces!" which may or may not be a true statement. Towards the landward end of the mole a considerable length of it becomes a viaduct, and was carried on open steel piling, so as to leave a clear waterway for tidal purposes. The mole was defended by artillery (Plate 21) as well as by machine-guns, and the execution which these, especially the latter, did on our brave fellows in the attack is still fresh in our minds.

PLATE XIX.

THE BRUGES CANAL.

The Canal which runs from Bruges to the sea at Zeebrugge, and which formed a chief access for the German submarines to the Channel. The concrete submarine shelters at Bruges remained undestroyed until the end of the war.

PLATE XX.

LOCK GATE AT ZEEBRUGGE.

One of the sliding caissons which formed the lock gates of the Canal at its Zeebrugge end. The dock into which the caisson slides to open the lock can be seen beyond the little footbridge.

PLATE XXI.
ON THE MOLE.

Two of the guns still standing on the Mole at Zeebrugge near its outer end.

PLATE XXII.

THE MOLE AT ZEEBRUGGE.

The inner side of the Mole at Zeebrugge, showing the part of the structure which was a viaduct carried on steel piles. The two heavy concrete piers were erected by the Germans to make the Mole again usable after the destruction caused by the exploded submarine.

It was, of course, against the open part of the structure, the steel viaduct, that Lieutenant Sandford steered his old submarine, full of explosives, with the object of blowing up the viaduct, and so preventing any help from the landward side getting to the men who were resisting our landing farther on. The viaduct is said to have been covered with soldiers watching the approach of C 3, and unsuspecting their fate. The boat was rammed into the structure, the Lieutenant and his crew got away safely, the fuse did its duty, the viaduct disappeared with everyone on it, and communication with the land was cut off. Plate 22 shows the viaduct, seen from the bend of the mole on the inner side, looking shorewards. The two concrete blocks supporting the landward end of the viaduct were, of course, built by the Germans after the attack—they show exactly the place where C 3 did its work. Plate 23 was taken from the outer side of the mole, and shows the present temporary viaduct on its concrete piers, and in deep water beside it a flagstaff carrying a white ensign which has been placed on the spot, very charmingly, by the Belgians, as a memorial of the pluck of the men who, under that flag, carried out the great exploit.

IV.—THE LYS SALIENT

(PLATES 24 TO 34.)

THE region between the Ypres Salient and the La Bassée Canal, extending from the high ground by Wytschaete and Messines to Kemmel and then south-westwards by Bailleul and Meteren to Merville, and finally sharply eastwards to Festubert and Givenchy, forms the ground which the German advance in April, 1918, made into the "Lys Salient," which was to have opened the way for them to the Channel ports, and to have cut the Allied Armies in two.

Neuve Chapelle lies on the main road four miles north of La Bassée, near the southern end of what became the Lys Salient later on, and was the scene of the first great action in March, 1915, after the hold-up by the mud of the winter. It had been lost very early in the war, and was regained after heavy fighting and great losses on both sides. The German papers complained characteristically that our artillery firing "was not war—it was murder"! All counter-attacks failed to recover it for the Germans, but, on the other hand, our own troops were not able to make any further advance towards the higher ground, known to us as the Aubers Ridge, which lay between them and Lille. After the attack the reports told us that two crucifixes still remained standing. One was at the cross-roads, and has since fallen or been removed. The other (Plate 24) was in the churchyard, and is still standing, with a dud shell embedded in its shaft. The village itself, like all the others, has disappeared; my photograph was taken from a heap of stones which represented what was left of the church. An attack in May made a valiant attempt to carry the Aubers Ridge, and some detachments succeeded in getting close to the Lille suburbs, but the ground could not be held. It was on this ground, at Escobecques, about six miles from Lille, that I found the late German Divisional H.Q. in farm-buildings fortified with something like 2,000 tons of reinforced concrete. "Bauern Gefecht Stelle" seems to have been the name of the buildings when in German occupation—"Fin de la Guerre" has come from the French. The "ridge" is by no means visible as a ridge, but is shown by the contours as a stretch of country from 30 to 50 feet higher than its surroundings. The deserted and blown-up pillboxes (Plate 18) of reinforced concrete are very much in evidence here, as they are farther north in the Passchendaele region, and the villages are often quite destroyed. But where the land has not been keenly fought over the shell and trench damage is not considerable, and cultivation is being carried on actively. At La Fresnoy, on the higher part of the ridge, a farm known to our people as "Somerset Farm" was utilised by the Germans as an O.P. (Plate 25) and a light signal station. An engraved stone tablet on the wall (barely visible on the right of the photograph) records that it is the "Schultze Turm," and that it was built in six weeks—certainly an excellent record. The O.P. tower still stands, a fine piece of solid construction, although the barn within which it was built, and which must have effectually concealed it, is a good deal damaged. Plate 26 shows, for comparison, a British double O.P. which I found standing (and which probably still stands) not far from La Bassée. The concrete and brick towers have resisted all attempts at their entire destruction, but the buildings which must originally have enclosed and concealed the towers appear only as heaps of brick rubbish.

In April, 1918, the German advance on the Lys—which, like its predecessors, succeeded all too nearly, but just not quite enough—and which proved to be Ludendorff's final despairing effort, started at Neuve Chapelle, then held by the Portuguese, who were to have been withdrawn the next day. The troops were hopelessly outnumbered, and gave way at once under the attack, and the British divisions right and left of them were uncovered. Givenchy and Festubert held firm[15] and Bethune was saved, but farther north everything gave way.

It was at this critical time that Haig issued the famous order which indicated at once the serious nature of the situation and the General's confidence in his troops:

"There is no other course open to us but to fight it out. Every position must be held to the last man; there must be no retirement. With our backs to the wall, and believing in the justice of our cause, each one of us must fight to the end. The safety of our homes and the freedom of mankind depend alike upon the conduct of each one of us at this critical moment."

It must have been the greatest of trials to the General to be compelled to order retirements a few days later on, but he had not deceived himself as to the quality of his men: they did fight to the end—fought the enemy to a standstill first, and later on drove him back over all the country he had overrun.

Estaires was taken on the next day and Merville two days later, this town forming the farthest progress westward in the April advance. An interesting note in Haig's Despatch[16] says:

"There is evidence that the German troops that had entered Merville had got out of hand, and instead of pressing their advantage wasted valuable time in plundering the town. On the 12th the 5th Division arrived and secured this front."

PLATE XXIII.

"C 3."

The outer side of the Zeebrugge Mole at the place where "C 3" was driven against it and blown up on St. George's Day, in 1918. The white ensign forms a graceful remembrance, on the part of the Belgians, of Lieutenant Sandford's great exploit.

Finally the Ypres Salient was almost wiped out (the enemy was within a mile and a half of the city), Armentières and Bailleul, Wytschaete and Messines, had to be evacuated, and the Lys Salient came into existence. Mount Kemmel was taken on the 25th, the French, overwhelmed, dying without surrendering. An advance of about ten miles had been made by the Germans over a very considerable distance, and over country which was of enormous importance to the Allies. North of Ypres, happily, the Belgians had been able to stand firm, and recovered at once, by counter-attacks, a small area on which they had had to give way. But once more sheer exhaustion, probably hastened by rashness after what must have been the unexpected success of the first onslaught, helped to bring the enemy to a stand, while the splendid stand of the Belgians to the north and our Territorials at Festubert and on the canal at Givenchy indicated clearly enough that no further advance could be gained. The fighting died down for two or three days, and then at last came the crucial attack, directed north-westwards across a line from Meteren to Voormezeele, where French and British were fighting side by side "with their backs to the wall." The attack failed, and on the next morning the

German lines were considerably farther back than they had been at the start. This proved to be the real end of the fighting, and only minor changes in the lines due to our advances and those of the French occurred until our final advance. Towards the end of July, when the great attack of Foch from the Marne to the Aisne had declared itself, the Germans commenced a withdrawal of their stores from the Lys Salient. Merville and Estaires had both been knocked about very much by our artillery during the German occupation. Merville was retaken on the 19th of August, and after that date our advance, and the retreat of the Germans, went on continuously. Kemmel Hill was again in the hands of the Allies by the 5th of September, and by the 6th the Lys Salient had disappeared. "Plug Street" Wood and Messines were cleared of the German rearguards on the 29th of September, at the time when Belgian and British troops together were finally annihilating the Ypres Salient, and succeeding in forty-eight hours in covering ground which had required four months in 1917. Armentières was again in our possession early in October.

Plates 27 to 32 are photographs of places which became of special interest—and anxiety—while the Germans were succeeding in creating the "Lys Salient." Merville (Plate 27) and Estaires (Plate 28) were totally wrecked by us while they were in German occupation, but with them, as with Bailleul (Plate 29), reconstruction is going on rapidly. Agricultural operations in this area are going on vigorously, and the damage was chiefly confined to the villages and little towns. The western half of Armentières had been pretty thoroughly rebuilt between my visits of 1919 and 1920, but the eastern half (Plate 30) was still largely ruinous.

The top of Kemmel Hill is about 350 feet higher than Ypres, and looks from the salient—even at a distance of seven to eight miles—as quite a little mountain. Plate 31 is a view taken from north of "Plug Street" Wood, about three miles from the hill, and Plate 32[17] was taken on the hill itself near the top. The hill was originally largely covered with woods, but only groups of bare stems are now remaining.

On the way from Armentières to Plug Street we found the ruins of a little estaminet, within which an O.P. of 1914 had been constructed by Colonel Gill. Towers with walls 3 feet thick had not been thought of in those days, and the light steel framework of the O.P. stood up, spidery, above the brick rubbish. At a farmhouse still standing across the road it was interesting to find a kindly French peasant woman who had now been able to return to her house, where she had stayed with her family for six months during the earlier fighting, living in the cellar. Her children seemed to cherish affectionate recollections of a certain kindly English "Capitaine Frederic," who was "rouge" and who gave them chocolates, and whom by these particulars I was afterwards able to identify. I suppose we are likely always to call Ploegsteert

"Plug Street." The village is, of course, in ruins, but the wood, of which Plate 33 shows only a corner, is too large to have been totally destroyed like the woods north of the Somme. At "Hyde Park Corner" (there were several "Hyde Park Corners" in Flanders) one came across the sight, only too familiar in many parts of the war area, of a British cemetery (Plate 34). It had been carefully tended and looked after, as we found to be always the case.

PLATE XXIV.

NEUVE CHAPELLE.

Two crucifixes remained standing at Neuve Chapelle after the Action of March, 1915. One of them has disappeared; the one photographed stands in what must have been the churchyard. A dud shell has split the shaft without bringing it down.

PLATE XXV.

ON THE AUBERS RIDGE.

The Schultze Turm, a very substantial German O.P. enclosed in "Somerset Farm." An inscription states that it was built in six weeks.

PLATE XXVI.

AN O.P.

A British double O.P. between Bethune and La Bassée. The buildings which once concealed it lie round it in a heap, but the towers have still some substance.

PLATE XXVII.

MERVILLE.

The farthest west point reached in the Lys Salient during the German advance in April, 1918. The town was practically destroyed by our shell-fire during the German occupation.

PLATE XXVIII.

ESTAIRES.

Like Merville, which lies four miles west of it, Estaires was terribly damaged by our shelling during its occupation by the Germans from April to August, 1918.

PLATE XXIX.

BAILLEUL.

Not to be confused with the village of the same name north of Arras, close to the Vimy Ridge. It was thoroughly ruined by the fighting in both directions during 1918.

PLATE XXX.

ARMENTIÈRES.

In 1919 very little had been done by way of reconstruction in Armentières, but a year later the western half of the town had been largely rebuilt, although the other half was still in the condition shown in the photograph.

PLATE XXXI.

KEMMEL HILL.

This photograph was taken from a distance of three miles, from which, however, the hill looks hardly as bold as it does from the higher part of the Menin Road. Its summit is about 350 feet higher than Ypres, which it entirely commands.

PLATE XXXII.

KEMMEL HILL.

The upper part of the hill itself, which was once largely covered with trees of which only the stems remain. It was captured, after an heroic French defence, in April, 1918, and held until the final retreat of the Germans began four months afterwards.

PLATE XXXIII.

"PLUG STREET" WOOD.

Ploegsteert will probably be "Plug Street" for all time in this country. Many trees are still standing in the wood. The turning to the left is the road to Messines.

PLATE XXXIV.

A CEMETERY AT "PLUG STREET."

A Royal Berks Military Cemetery at the north-east corner of "Plug Street" Wood.

PLATE XXXV.

BETHUNE.

The lighter-coloured masonry halfway up the fine old tower shows where houses were standing built closely round it. Their debris has been entirely cleared away and the Grande Place is as tidy as it is, unhappily, empty.

V.—BETHUNE, LA BASSÉE, AND LOOS

(PLATES 35 TO 42.)

THE pleasant little town of Bethune, with its friendly, Scotch-like name, lies just beyond the coal district, a dozen miles north-west of Lens and seven miles west of La Bassée. Our front lines during most of the war crossed the Bethune-La Bassée road about the line of Festubert and Givenchy, two and a half miles short of La Bassée. Although so near the German lines, it was not seriously shelled until the attempted German advance in March and April, 1918, when in two months the whole centre of the town was reduced to ruins. Colonel Gill, taking me through it a few months later, had some difficulty even in recognising "Bond Street," which for years had been a tolerably safe place for buying tobacco, or visiting a barber, or taking lunch, or meeting friends. We walked over 2 feet of brick débris along what must have been the roadway. The outlying parts of the town are comparatively little damaged. The fourteenth-century belfry tower (Plate 35) was closely encircled by houses, built up against it, which have altogether disappeared, and the tower itself shows hideous cracks over practically its whole height. The Church of St. Vaast is so completely destroyed that one can only tell one end from the other by the orientation of its site.

In the great German attack of April, 1918, the town was saved by the Lancashires when the Portuguese had failed us near Neuve Chapelle, and when we were compelled to give way from Armentières to Merville, a few miles farther north. The same troops ("second-rate troops" the Germans called them) held Givenchy, on the La Bassée Canal. The village has entirely disappeared. Plate 36 was taken from a mound on which I believe that the church once stood (but there were not even stones visible on the surface to mark the place), looking back over the British lines. Lord Haig[18] tells how two batteries each left a gun within 500 yards of the draw-bridge at Givenchy, and, assisted by a party of gunners who held the bridge with rifles, succeeded in stopping the German advance at this most critical time.

The country between Bethune and La Bassée and northwards and southwards for miles from that line, was in 1919 a desert, bare of trees, of houses, of crops, of people, growing nothing but shell craters and barbed wire, with thousands of tons of buried broken shells likely to be very offensive to agricultural implements! The seven miles of road between the two towns runs eastward through the desolation, never very far south of the canal, and at Cuinchy close to the brickfields and the "railway triangle," the scene of specially hard fighting in 1915. The triangle again defeated our attack in September, 1916.

The little town of La Bassée (Plate 37), the name of which was for long so familiar to us, is, of course, a heap of ruins. I remember a statement in a German paper in 1914 to the effect that, La Bassée and the canal (Plate 38, which shows a reconstructed bridge) being in their hands, their final success was quite assured! The eight miles of road from La Bassée to Lens passes Hulloch and Loos and Hill 70, and enters Lens by the Cité St. Laurent, a suburb which was in our hands long before we were in the town itself. The road from Bethune to Lens passes between Loos and the "Double Crassier." The ruined pithead (Plate 39) near Hulloch is only an example of the condition to which the Germans reduced all the colliery workings in the district on which they could lay hands.

The story of the great fights at Loos is full of splendid episodes, although the results of the fighting were very much less than had been hoped for. In April, 1915, the German front lay from a point west of Loos and Lens southward nearly as far as Arras, covering the colliery villages and the Lorette and Vimy Ridges. It was first broken by the great attack in 1915, which gave the French all the Lorette Ridge except its extreme east end. Opposite Loos, across the Lens-Béthune road, lay the twin slag heaps known as the Double Crassier (Plate 40), where for many months the opposing front trenches were literally within a few yards of each other, the Germans holding the slag heaps. There are stories of mutual courtesies and jocularity between Saxons and our own men under these conditions, which came to an end (from the German side) when Prussians replaced Saxons. But if the trenches had been in our Midlands, with Yorkshire laid waste beyond them, instead of in a foreign country, probably our boys would have felt differently. We did not hear of, or expect to hear of, any similar friendliness where the French poilus were concerned. Farther north came the strongly fortified "Fosse No. 8" and the Hohenzollern Redoubt close to Haisnes, and just short of the canal at Givenchy. What we got to know as the Loos battle began on the 25th of September, 1915. The Double Crassier was taken at once. A man in the London Irish is said to have kicked off a football from the parapet in this attack and dribbled it across No Man's Land to the German first lines.[19] The Hohenzollern Redoubt was penetrated, the Highlanders got to the northern suburbs of Lens, and the front line passed to the east of the Lens-La Bassée road. But further progress became impossible, and early in October our front line was for the time "stabilised" west of the road. The great redoubt still remained practically in German hands. In this fighting the 47th Division London Territorials took part, the first complete Cockney division to take the field.

PLATE XXXVI.

GIVENCHY.

The British positions at Givenchy, north of the La Bassée Canal, looking back from the site of the village. The holding of these positions in April, 1918, prevented Ludendorff's final attack from reaching Bethune.

PLATE XXXVII.

LA BASSÉE.

The ruined village as it was left, when the roadways were cleared, after the evacuation by the Germans in their retreat in 1918.

PLATE XXXVIII.

THE LA BASSÉE CANAL.

The temporary lifting bridge over the canal at La Bassée. The buildings are, of course, reconstruction. The German newspapers proclaimed that the capture of the canal here, in 1915, made the result of the war quite certain!

PLATE XXXIX.

A PITHEAD.

Pithead work near Hulloch—a fair example of the state to which all pit works in the district were reduced before the Germans left.

Of the Loos episodes there will not be forgotten that which got Piper Laidlaw, of the 7th K.O.S.B., his V.C., for marching up and down on the parapet (close to the Cité St. Laurent, a suburb of Lens) with his pipes until all the men were out of the trenches, and carrying on until he was himself wounded. Nor will it be easily forgotten how Mdlle. Moreau, the daughter of a miner, devoted herself, during the first German occupation, to saving and nursing British wounded soldiers, or how later on, when we arrived there, she met our entering troops and, obtaining a rifle, was able to shoot sundry German soldiers who were attacking wounded men. She lost father and brother during the war. One is glad to know that she was awarded the Croix de Guerre, and that some of the soldiers, to whose welfare she was so devoted, regardless of her own safety, have bought land at Bethune and built a little house on it where she can carry on business, which one hopes will be most successful.

The zigzag communication trench, which will be familiar to many of our soldiers (Plate 41), forms a bit of roadside scenery typical of the country here over which the fighting went on in 1915 and for long afterwards. Loos itself was afterwards handed over to the French, who were not, unfortunately, able to retain it. Just beyond Loos, after it had been regained in 1918, I was stumbling over a bit of ground covered with all sorts of débris beside what had been lately German trenches, and which was even then being occasionally enviously shelled, when I saw growing in a crevice below the brick rubbish a garden pansy. I was, no doubt, walking over some cottager's garden, but garden and cottage were all now the same and all equally unrecognisable. The bright little flower, blowing uninjured at the bottom of its rubbish heap, seemed a pleasant emblem of the freeing and recovery of France which was just then coming so near.

Near to my discovery of the heartsease I found some of Colonel Gill's men in charge of a height-finder. They had comfortable enough quarters in a German dugout in which I found, and secured as a prize, a little booklet left behind by its late occupants. It is entitled "Wer da?" ("Who goes there?"), and contains a dozen chapters of a very pious and didactic kind on the duties of a soldier, his oath, his honour, his religion, and so on. The chapter on "Der Kriegsherr und der Eid" is rather pathetic in view of subsequent events. Here is a paragraph from it:

"It is thoroughly *altergermanisch* and entirely in correspondence with the character of the German people to follow a King, who represents the might of God in earthly things ... who is a father to his country and a guide and war-lord to his soldiers. Between this prince and the soldiers there exists the most special and intimate relationship. He is the head and the heart of the Army; it is his shield and his sword. It protects his rights and his sacred person. He cares for it and shares its troubles and dangers."

What a cynical comment on this sort of stuff that the precious Kriegsherr ran away from his country and his beloved army a few weeks later! Then, again:

"We speak of '*deutscher Treue.*' It is a national heirloom handed down to us from our ancestors.... It shows itself through unbreakable adherence to the oath the soldier has made to his Fürsten und Kriegsherrn!"

Presumably this particular oath did not belong to the category of scraps of paper. Ninety-eight pages out of the hundred of which the book consists are devoted to this sort of statement and exhortation. But it is only fair to the reverend author to mention that, on the last two pages, under the heading "*Im Krieg*," he enjoins consideration, as a matter of "*Christliche Liebe*," for the people of the conquered countries, ending by an emphatic warning that the soldiers should think what would happen to their homes if the enemy were not imbued with the same Christian spirit! Unfortunately, this not very exalted motive for decent behaviour did not prove itself sufficiently vigorous to have any effect on the people whose parsons had gloried in the "merriness of war" four years earlier, when they thought that the fighting would be over and their own side victorious in a couple of months.

When one passes beside or over miles of No Man's Land, such as looks picturesque enough in Plate 42, one has to remember that one is not seeing a miniature landscape of chalk hills, such as would delight any youngster on Hampstead Heath, but seeing, perhaps, a garden, perhaps a cottage home, an orchard, a piece of green meadow, turned into ruin by the Huns. Surely the ghosts of these inanimate things must haunt, with the ghosts of thousands of innocent men, the people who turned their neighbour's country, animate and inanimate, from a joyful and living reality into wilderness and a graveyard!

PLATE XL.

THE DOUBLE CRASSIER.

In front of the two long spoil heaps which went by this name the opposing trenches were for a long time within a few yards of each other. The Double Crassier was taken by us in the Loos battle of September, 1915.

PLATE XLI.

A COMMUNICATION TRENCH.

A British Communication Trench near Loos. The rising ground in the distance is a part of the Lorette Ridge.

PLATE XLII.

"NO MAN'S LAND."

Between Hulloch and Lens, a fair example of the destroyed pasture land where the churned-up chalk was too near the surface for the growth of the weedy vegetation such as appears in Plates XVII and XVIII.

PLATE XLIII.

ARRAS.

The central part of Arras seen from a height. The photograph shows what a town looks like even when it is, compared to others, not very badly destroyed!

VI.—ARRAS, VIMY, AND LENS

(PLATES 43 TO 50.)

ARRAS was in the possession of the Germans for three days in September, 1914, but they evacuated it in their retreat after the first battle of the Marne. It was only by very plucky fighting, however, that the French were able to keep them even a mile or two away, and for a long time they remained at St. Laurent-Blangy, which is practically in the north-eastern suburbs of the town. In October, 1914, therefore, they were only a couple of miles away, and from this short distance the centre of the city was bombarded severely by heavy artillery. The beautiful Hôtel de Ville and the belfry were destroyed, and the centre of the city generally much injured, as the view from above (Plate 43, an official photograph) shows very painfully. In April, 1916, the British being then in this zone, Arras was practically "cleared," the enemy being forced backwards for six miles. In the offensive of March, 1918, the Germans succeeded in getting two miles closer in on the south, but to the north the 1916 positions were held, and the enemy was finally driven twelve miles away towards Cambrai in our August offensive in 1918.

Outside the centre of the city the damage did not appear—when I first visited it while it was still under occasional long-range shell-fire—to be nearly so great as in the centre. Many houses were standing and at least more or less habitable, if windowless, and a few poor shops in the outskirts had started business. But published statistics indicate that more than half the houses are damaged beyond possibility of reconstruction. The cathedral, which is altogether in ruins (Plate 44), is an eighteenth-century basilica, and is happily not one of the glories of France. Some of the columns of the main arcade, standing by themselves with a piece of architrave still remaining in place, reminded one a little of the two beautiful Roman columns still standing on the stage of the theatre at Arles. A notice stood beside the ruins in 1918—I think it is still there—to the effect that it was intended to leave them unrestored to form an enduring reminder of the Huns. I hope it is not disrespectful for a great lover of French Gothic architecture to say that probably this particular building may really be more impressive in its ruined condition than it can ever have been when it was standing.

It was really remarkable to find in 1919 that the half-ruined town was already full of people going to and from the station, and obviously doing their best to carry on in spite of the surrounding conditions. We lunched at an hotel showing very many signs of dilapidation, but obviously serving a very considerable number of customers—quite a cheering sight.

I am not likely soon to forget a drive from Cambrai to Arras, on a very dark night, by by-roads which our Engineers had not yet visited, and while traffic regulations still prohibited even the very feeble illumination which could be obtained from an official headlamp. But the discomfort was much mitigated by the pleasure of watching a fine display of miscellaneous coloured fires to the south of our line, due to the discovery by our Tommies that the Germans had left large stores of signal lights behind in their retreat!

On from Arras to Cambrai runs the road which is the continuation of the Cambrai-Le Cateau road. It goes straight and level over fine rolling uplands like a Scotch moor, but with grass and herbage instead of heather, and (in 1918) with endless craters, trenches, and entanglements, and no hills in sight except the ridges away to the north left far behind.

The Vimy Ridge (Plate 45) rises at Bailleul, five miles north-east of Arras, and continues in a north-westerly direction for about the same distance to Givenchy.[20] It is steep on its eastern side and gently sloping on the western, and the highest part of the ridge is about 200 feet above the lower land to the east. The height is not great, but is amply sufficient to give the forces occupying it complete observation over the surrounding country in all directions. I was on it first on a brilliant afternoon in 1918, when the Germans were still trying to make a stand a little east of Lens. Away somewhere in the direction of Douai a great explosion was followed by a column of white smoke, brilliant in the sunshine, and spreading out into a huge white flower 3,000 feet above the ground—clearly a huge German "dump" blown up to prevent it falling into our hands. Below us a battery of field-guns was pounding away at the German lines, still only two or three miles beyond them. A German 'plane came in sight, engaged in the singularly futile business of dropping "propaganda" literature from a height which kept it out of the reach of 13-pounders. From away over Lens, where under a dark cloud the Germans were still trying, in despair, to avoid their Nemesis, came the dull noise of the fighting. Behind the ridge lay the shell-marked slopes up which the Canadians rushed in April, 1917, and from which afterwards even the wild German push of a year later failed to move us. In the distance behind the ridge towards the west stood the tower of Mont St. Eloi, battered about in fighting from the fifteenth century to the nineteenth; and having now again seen the Prussians on the soil of its country, and surely rejoicing—even as inanimate masonry—when at last "der Tag" had arrived, and the land had become once more its own, with peace and victory not far away.

The capture of the somewhat higher Lorette Ridge (a continuation of the Vimy Ridge across the gap at Souchez) in 1915 was one of the finest achievements of the French Army; the position was enormously strong and most stiffly defended. The ridge, with its commanding observation to the north, was held against all counter-attacks until the war was over. The northern portion of the Vimy Ridge, however, which was taken at the same time, could not be held. It was eventually taken by the Canadians in April, 1917, under General Byng (now Lord Byng "of Vimy"), after great preparations, for its possession by the Germans had put us under much disadvantage. Mining operations on a very great scale formed part of the scheme of attack. [Plate 46](#) is a view of one of the largest of the mine craters on the ridge above Neuville St. Vaast, near the elaborate defences known as the "Labyrinth." The well-concealed German gun-emplacements below the ridge (of which [Plate 47](#) shows one of a number at Thelus) had given us great trouble and caused much loss. They were all taken with the ridge, and henceforth the guns from Vimy fired in the opposite direction.

Over the country, *très accidentée*, west of the ridge one might have thought oneself, in 1918, as in some queerly altered part of England. At all the principal road-crossings men in khaki regulated the traffic, everywhere were conspicuous public notices in English, and in the villages the shops exhibited signs such as "Tommy's House," "Entrée libre," or—very frequently—"Eggs and Chips." But driving eastwards through this green and pleasant country and the busy villages one came with startling suddenness and with a drawing of one's breath upon the wilderness. Here, just as north and east of Amiens, villages ceased to be; only disconnected bits of brickwork and general ruin were left, very often not even so much, and nothing but a large painted signboard with a name on it gave any indication whatever of the site of a village. Gardens and fields were all one mass of ragged, chalky shell-holes overgrown with hateful-looking weeds. Trees had disappeared. Only the roads themselves had been engineered into something like decent condition by the levelling up of shell-holes and the clearing away to the sides of brick and timber débris. At a later time the timber had been utilised either for construction or for firing, and the bricks were being systematically cleaned and trimmed and stacked for use in the reconstruction that has been continued since with ever-increasing rapidity.

The villages—Gavrelle and others—on the Valenciennes road east of Arras are practically blotted out, but the towns farther east, which were out of the fighting area, are not much, if at all, damaged structurally. But no doubt the Germans either destroyed or stole all the machinery and industrial appliances they could lay their hands on, in the benevolent desire to ruin French industry for the benefit of their own, for which Lille and Tournai and Roubaix have had to pay so dearly.

From Arras to Lens runs northward the ten miles of straight road, crossing the Vimy Ridge on the way ([Plate 48](#)), down which our people must have so often looked on the little town which, until the very end of the war, resisted all attempts of our Allies or of ourselves to enter it. The photograph was taken from outside Lens, looking towards the ridge, which forms the higher ground in the distance.

Lens itself, a prosperous little town having in 1914 some 28,000 inhabitants, in the centre of the French coal-mining district, is one of the many places which, unimportant even within its own country and quite unknown beyond it, has now become a name familiar over the whole world. It was occupied by the Germans in October, 1914, and was almost continually fought for until the British finally entered it four years later. It became eventually the centre of a very narrow salient which covered even its suburbs, but the town itself, drenched with gas and horrible to stay in, held out bravely to the end.

The town is destroyed as thoroughly as Ypres, and more completely than any other place in France. Some idea of the state of Lens early in 1919 is given by Mr. Basil Mott's photograph (Plate 49), taken when it was under snow.

The town is too large to be entirely wiped out, as the villages are, and converted into chalk-pits and shell-holes. But standing on the mound which once was the Church of St. Léger, or on any other point of vantage, one saw in 1919 nothing but a waste of bricks and stones and timber (Plate 50), with no semblance of standing buildings beyond the sheds which had been put up in some space sufficiently cleared to allow of their erection. If one had not seen so much appalling destruction in so many places it would have been unbelievable that a town larger than Bedford or Doncaster should be as entirely turned into small fragments as if some gigantic harrow had been drawn across it.

In 1920 I found that a considerable amount of rebuilding had taken place, although still by far the greater part of the town remained in ruins.

To the west of Lens, northwards and southwards, the whole country is given up to coal-mining. The mines, as everyone knows, were destroyed wantonly, and with great thoroughness, by the Germans. It must be years before they can be working fully again, but the French have not lost much time in taking steps to reinstate them. Even while fighting was still going on a few miles away, I found that in a large colliery near Givenchy (Liévin), where an "Archy" section was at work, and where the whole of the buildings and the pithead work were a mass of ruins, pumping machinery was already at work, and the water pumped up was being utilised in the neighbourhood.

In 1920 a good many of the pits were actually at work, and on the roads one welcomed the familiar sight of miners going to and from their work. The colliery villages (Liévin is nearly as large as Lens) had at first sight a very deceptive appearance of substantiality, but closer inspection showed that what seemed to be uninjured terraces of cottages were nothing much more than bare and roofless walls. Later on one found these ruins being blown up in order to clear the ground, as well as to provide bricks for rebuilding.

General Haig adopted in this neighbourhood, in 1917, a system of feint attacks which he describes as quite successful in their object, although they had the disadvantage that they frequently prevented him from denying German accounts of the bloody repulse of British attacks which in fact had never occurred at all! The most noteworthy of these feint attacks took place near Liévin, as to which he says:—

"On this occasion large numbers of dummy men and some dummy tanks were employed, being raised up at zero hour by pulling ropes. These dummies drew a heavy fire and were shot to pieces. The Germans duly reported that an attack had been annihilated, and that rows of British dead could be seen lying before our lines."[21]

From Lens eastwards towards Lille the surface destruction diminishes rapidly. Trees have been cut down (probably in 1918), but cultivation seems to have gone on uninterruptedly—for the benefit of the invader, of course—during the war.

PLATE XLIV.

ARRAS CATHEDRAL.

Ruins which it has been proposed to leave in their present condition, if they will stand, as a memorial of the once too near neighbourhood of the Germans.

PLATE XLV.

THE VIMY RIDGE.

This Ridge, between Arras and Lens, is several miles in length, and over 200 feet above the surrounding country. Its possession was therefore of extraordinary value for observation and artillery purposes. We captured it in April, 1917, and the Germans were never able to recover it. The very similar Lorette Ridge, taken earlier by the French, forms a continuation of it some six miles long, towards the north-west.

PLATE XLVI.

A MINE CRATER.

One of the mine craters blown on the Vimy Ridge as a first step in the attack which captured the Ridge in 1917.

PLATE XLVII.

AT THELUS.

One of the German gun emplacements on the north of the Vimy Ridge which, being outside our direct observation, made it so important that the Ridge should be taken.

PLATE XLVIII.

THE ROAD TO LENS.

From the Vimy Ridge (seen in the distance in the photograph) our men could look straight along the four miles of road to Lens; but it was eighteen months after the capture of the Ridge that they actually got possession of what was left of the town.

PLATE XLIX.

LENS UNDER SNOW.

The wilderness that was once Lens, as it appeared early in 1919.

PLATE L.

LENS.

Later on in 1919 some sheds and temporary buildings were to be seen wherever space had been cleared for their erection. Another visit some months later showed that very much progress had been made in the way of reconstruction, but of course, as a whole, the town is still a mass of ruins.

VII.—THE SOMME

(PLATES 51 TO 66.)

I have been able to traverse several times since the war the great stretch of country in Picardy which is generally spoken of at home as "the Somme"—country over which much of our hardest fighting took place in 1916 and 1918, and where thousands of our brave men are now lying. We became only too familiar with the names of places within it, which might have peacefully remained for centuries more in the happy oblivion in which they had rested for centuries past, had not the war waves broken upon them and destroyed them while making them immortal. Much of the country had been so completely devastated that there was nothing in it or on it to show in a picture—nothing beyond an irregular expanse of ground broken everywhere into shell-holes and covered over with an untidy wild herbage of rank weeds. But the interest of this country to all of us at home—and "at home" in this case more than ever includes the homes overseas—is so close and so poignant that it is probably worth while to add here some little description of the characteristics of the great area which we call "the Somme," and the positions of the places which we fought over.

In the thirty miles from Amiens to Péronne the Somme runs from east to west in a narrow valley, with eight immense double bends round spurs which project alternately from the higher country (some 200 feet above the river-level) on the north and south. The main road eastwards from Amiens lies south of the river, and rises gradually to the higher level at Villers Bretonneux, about ten miles from the city, and then continues dead straight and nearly level, till it drops again at Brie (twenty-nine miles from Amiens), to the Somme valley, after the river has taken its sharp bend to the south at Péronne, which is four miles north of Brie. As one goes eastwards from Amiens the route becomes more and more war-worn. At first the ordinary avenues of trees still stand, farther on the trees become fewer and fewer, and finally disappear entirely (Plate 51), and a region of total destruction is reached, where only rough indications remain of the sites of the villages.

But in 1919 I found German prisoners at work filling up shell-holes (the French and ourselves did not make prisoners dig front-line trenches), levelling the ground, and clearing up generally, and some reoccupation of land had already started, peasants and "store"-keepers living in such temporary bungalows as they could construct. Somehow or other the owners of different strips of land along the road seemed to have discovered which particular strip belonged to each one, ploughing was already going on, and cultivation had been started in quite a number of places.

The river itself lies always too low down in its valley to be visible from the road, from which the view to the north looks right over to the high ground between the Somme and the Ancre. The Avre, coming from Montdidier and Moreuil in the south, falls into the Somme close to Amiens, and the Ancre, coming from Albert in the north, joins the main river at Corbie, four miles north of Villers Bretonneux.

Albert is about eighteen miles north-east of Amiens by a straight road through Pont Noyelles, which continues to Bapaume, eleven miles farther. On the high ground between the Ancre and the Albert-Bapaume road stood Thiepval and the German redoubts, and on the Bapaume road itself Pozières, Courcelette, and Warlencourt.

In the angle between the Albert-Bapaume road and the northern bank of the Somme every village and every wood became part of a tragic history— Mametz, Contalmaison, Longueval, Guillemont, Combles, with Trones Wood, Delville Wood, and the others. South of the Somme and between the river and the road lie Hamel and Chuignes, while on the main road itself, east of Villers Bretonneux, once stood the villages of Warfusée (Lamotte), Estrées, Villers Carbonnel, and others, while the town of Péronne— protected by Mont St. Quentin on the north and by the Somme and a tributary on the other three sides—lies just at the bend. South of the road and in the triangle between it and the Avre lie the uplands on which, very generally, the French were fighting to the right (south) of the British, and in which the village names are therefore less familiar to us than those farther north.

The first battle of the Somme commenced on the 1st of July, 1916, and lasted, with more or less quiescent intervals, until the late autumn. British and French were fighting side by side—the British on the northern half, from the Upper Ancre to the Albert-Péronne road; the French to their right, facing Péronne, crossing the Somme, and extending southward as far as Chaulnes.

The German defences in the north, which had been under construction for more than a year, were enormously strong, the "first line" alone being a maze of trenches half a mile wide.

Their position stretched southward from below Arras to Gommécourt, and covered Beaumont-Hamel and the heights east of the Ancre valley, crossed the Albert-Bapaume road two miles north of Albert, passed eastwards through Fricourt, crossed the Somme some miles short of Péronne, and then ran southwards west of Chaulnes. The story of the fighting, both French and British, as it can be read even in Lord Haig's official despatches, and still more in the unofficial accounts, is a continuous record of episodes every one of which would have been called Homeric in any other war, but which in this gigantic struggle seem to have become ordinary events. The ordinary civilian of common life from workshop or warehouse or office or studio turned out to be in essence exactly the same being as the noble and adventurous heroes of the stories and histories of our youth. And while he would grumble seriously about his baths or his meat or his shaving facilities, he would yet go into action cheerfully without hesitation, although he knew well enough the horror of his own work and the great chance that he might never return.

The village of Mametz (Plate 53), like nearly all the villages in "the Somme," has disappeared; it was among those taken by the British on the first day of the battle. It was in this attack that East Surrey men are said to have gone forward dribbling footballs, some of which they recovered in German trenches, in front of them.[22]

The French on our right got within a mile or two of Péronne, but its defences were too strong and it was not actually captured until 1918.

Trones Wood (Plate 54) was cleared early in July. Here a small body of 170 men of the Royal West Kents and Queens[23] held out all night, completely surrounded, until relieved the next morning. Delville Wood (Plate 55) was captured the next day. The fighting in these woods has left nothing of them but churned-up ground and a few bare stems, although the rank undergrowth makes some of them appear quite green from a distance. Combles (Plate 56) was not taken until the 26th of September, when the British and French entered the town simultaneously (from the north and the south respectively), and captured a company which had not been able to get clear away in time. The little town is not so entirely wrecked as many other places, but the house which is shown under reconstruction in the photograph is perhaps one of the least damaged.

Thiepval and the redoubts on the Thiepval plateau were not finally secured until November. The Germans had said beforehand that we "would bite granite" in trying to take them. We did bite granite, but our teeth proved the harder.

Along the Albert-Bapaume road the villages of Pozières and Courcelette have disappeared altogether. Sometimes a big iron gate, or half a gate, or a stone gatepost, shows where an entrance once existed to some more or less pretentious mansion, but the building itself has gone entirely, and its site is grown over with rank herbage, which hides every indication even of where the house once stood. The whole Thiepval plateau is now a wilderness of weedy vegetation, and the weeds seem to have swallowed up the redoubts altogether, as well as Thiepval itself.

The defences on the Upper Ancre still barred the way to Bapaume along the road by Le Sars and the Butte de Warlencourt (Plate 57).[24] The Butte was the centre of the German position, as strongly protected by trenches and wire as even the Thiepval plateau itself. Fierce attacks in October and November, 1916, failed to secure it, and the chalky hillock was only finally taken in February, 1917. It now carries five crosses erected in memory of the units which fought there.

The mud, our chief enemy, made active operations impossible for a time. It was an even worse enemy than the Germans. General Haig says[25] that the trenches were channels of deep mud and the roads almost impassable, making all problems of supply most serious. General Maurice calls it, later on, a "morass of stinking mud." We were, in fact, at that time—and at other times as well—fighting the elements as well as the Germans. On the 17th of March, 1917, however (after the Warlencourt Ridge had been carried), Bapaume itself, which had been systematically destroyed by the Germans before they evacuated it, was at last entered.

Bapaume in 1919 was, like Albert, being rapidly reinhabited, and the new buildings (perhaps due to their being closer to the main road) were more in evidence than in most other places.

The villages north of Bapaume on the Arras road (Behagnies, Ervillers, and others) are, like those nearer the Somme, practically wiped out. But here, also, peasants and small shopkeepers were returning "home," and sheltering themselves as best they could in some sort of hutments.

On the 17th of March, 1917, also, the Germans having just commenced their great retirement, Mont St. Quentin was taken, and the next day Péronne itself. Plate 58 shows the dry bed of the Nord Canal where the road crosses it just at the rise on the back (north) of Mont St. Quentin. Plate 59 shows the ruin of the Church of St. Jean at Péronne. The little town itself, originally of about 5,000 inhabitants, was in parts systematically burnt and destroyed by mines by the Germans before they evacuated it in 1917, and further damaged by Franco-British shell-fire in 1918. On the spot I was told that the great church had been among the buildings deliberately burnt by the Germans; in any case it is now, like the rest of the town, a mere ruin. The outrages perpetrated by the Germans in their masterly retreat in 1917 extended across the whole area of the retirement (see Plate 119), and have been sufficiently described, so far as it has been possible in any decent paper to describe them. But the burnt and shattered houses were not the matters, bad as they were, which caused the intense feeling of loathing in addition to anger among the French, when they were at last able to return to their desecrated homes.

For a year after March, 1917, the Somme area ceased to be fought over, as the German retirement in 1917 had removed them far to the east. A year later the tables were turned, when on the 21st of March Ludendorff's great attack, cleverly directed against our weakest spot, began to drive us back from St. Quentin towards Amiens, and succeeded so rapidly that on the 23rd the Germans were at Péronne and on the 25th near Estrées, three miles east of the Somme on the Amiens road. On the 25th our Allies, on our right, had been compelled to fall back as far as Noyon. At this critical moment there was got together surely the most remarkable auxiliary force that a British General has ever had under his command. General Haig says:

"As the result of a conference on the 25th of March, a mixed force, including details, stragglers, schools personnel, tunnelling companies, army troops companies, field survey companies, and Canadian and American Engineers, had been got together and organised by General Grant, the Chief Engineer to the Fifth Army."[26]

The line on which this "mixed force" was placed passed through Warfusée (Plate 60). Some of the men collected were Engineer civilians with no previous training, and no knowledge of rifle-shooting. I have been told that they were pronounced most plucky, "but somewhat dangerous"! In the result, however, they did yeoman service in helping to hold back the onslaught until the distant reserves could arrive and until the attackers had eventually exhausted themselves.

On the next day came the historic conference at Doullens, which resulted in the appointment of General Foch in supreme control of the united forces (p. 3). But General Haig found it necessary to withdraw his troops still farther, and the German advance was finally checked only at Warfusée-Ablancourt, some ruins of which appear in Plate 60. The enemy never succeeded in reaching the crest of the high ground from which he could so completely have commanded Amiens (p. 38), although he was able to hold Villers Bretonneux, after a new attack on the 24th of April, for a few hours, after which he was turned out by the Anzacs and never got back. It was in this attack that British tanks met German tanks and beat them.

It was not until the 8th of August, 1918, after Foch had carried on his successful attacks on the Marne Salient for three weeks, that the great counter-attack on the Somme was fully started, although before that day there had been some important gains. Especially had a notable combination of Australians, Americans, and Tanks had a great success on the 4th of July, after a heavy barrage, in capturing Hamel, a village on the Somme just north of Warfusée. Both the Australians and the Tank Corps have given picturesque accounts of this fighting, with a somewhat amusing preference, in each case, for the service with which the writer is connected. It was here that the Australians are credited with having pronounced their new colleagues from across the Atlantic to be "good lads, but too rough"!

Most elaborate (and successful) precautions [27] had been taken to make sure that the attack of the 8th of August (Ludendorff's "black day") should be a surprise. In spite of all these precautions, some anxiety may have been felt by those who knew that a sergeant, who was well acquainted with everything that was on foot, had been taken prisoner by the Germans a few days before. Oddly enough, the minutes of the cross-examination of this N.C.O. were afterwards captured, and it was found that, like a plucky Englishman, he had given nothing whatever away.[28]

Villers Bretonneux had been throughout in our possession, but only its ruins were standing, the one "hotel" which I found there in 1919 being a tarpaulin-covered shed (Plate 61) calling itself the "Hôtel des Trois Moineaux," and bearing a cryptic message from "Toto" which I am unable to explain. The first day's advance swept far beyond Warfusée, just south of which the village of Marcelcave was captured by a tank whose Lieutenant demanded—and obtained—a receipt from the Australians before he would hand over his spoils to them. Abreast of Foucaucourt (Plate 52) and between it and the Somme lies Chuignes, where the Australian advance captured a 380-mm. gun on an elaborate emplacement, which had been put in position, but I believe too late to be used, for the purpose of a long-range bombardment of Amiens. The gun was dismantled before we reached it, and lies on the ground shorn of some 10 feet of its muzzle end, which had been cut off by its captors to send home as a "souvenir."

The Chipilly spur (Plate 62), north of Warfusée on the north side of the river, caused some heavy fighting, but was taken by the Londoners on the second day of the advance, with the help of two companies of Americans who are said to have lost touch with their own division and to have been quite ready to lend a hand in any fighting that was going on. The photograph gives some idea of the river itself at a place where it is navigable over a great breadth. Cappy (Plate 63) is a little farther upstream, where the river has divided itself into various channels, the particular one seen being the navigable canal, the rest of the river spreading over a quarter of a mile of marsh land to the north bank.

The land beside the Amiens-Péronne road becomes more and more ruined as one goes eastwards. Plate 51 shows something of what the actual road looks like, but no picture can indicate the state of the land itself, the country that was once fertile fields and farms. On my last visit (early in 1920) it was pleasant, but pathetic, to see that many peasants had somehow been able to find out which strip had been theirs before the war, and had built themselves hutments—they could hardly be called houses—in which they could at any rate live beside the land which they loved and which they are trying once more to cultivate. Towards Villers Carbonnel the countryside shows itself as more and more destroyed. Plate 64 (an officially taken photograph) indicates the appearance of that village immediately after we passed through it in 1918 and before the clearing-up work had commenced. A little later the broken woodwork would be collected for firing and the bricks from the fallen walls (if enough were left) would be trimmed and stacked ready for use again in making such dwellings as will anyhow make it possible for the peasants to get back again. In France they do not wait for trade union permissions, or "skilled" labour, or the sanitary (and other) regulations of County Councils, but go straight ahead and build. It seems certainly the best way of getting houses.

General Haig tells us how in March, 1917, when we were trying to keep up with the retreating Germans along this road, the part of it between Villers Carbonnel and the Somme at Brie was almost knee-deep in mud, so that it took the troops sixteen hours to cover the last four and a half miles. The difficulty of this crossing can be well understood by everyone who has seen the breadth and character of the flat marshy ground which, over a great part of the distance from Amiens, represents the bottom of the Somme valley. Some indication of the difficulty of troops crossing the river can be gathered from Plate 65, which is taken from below Cléry, close to the point at which the Australians crossed the river on the 31st of August, 1918, and made the magnificent attack on Mont St. Quentin, which resulted in the capture of Péronne the next day, and earned such warm praise from the Commander-in-Chief.[29]

The Château of Brie (Plate 66) lies on the Somme only half a mile south of the crossing of the main road from Amiens to St. Quentin, and therefore some four miles south of the great bend of the river at Péronne. On the 27th of September, 1918, it was the scene of a wonderful dress rehearsal for the crossing of the Hindenburg Line at the St. Quentin Canal two days later (see p. 58). Rafts, collapsible boats and life-lines, and some of the 3,000 life-belts which had been hurried up from the coast, were all tested, to make sure that there should be neither hesitation nor failure in their use in the attack on the "absolutely impregnable" section. And, as everyone knows, there *was* neither hesitation nor failure; the St. Quentin Canal was carried by the Terriers on the appointed day, and with this success, and the crossing of the "Kriemhilde" Line by the Americans in the middle of October, the last standing places for the retreating German armies vanished.

On the road east of the Somme from Brie to Péronne one saw a curious phenomenon which I seldom saw elsewhere, and cannot explain. In some way the trees in the felled avenue had been able to reassert their life, and for a considerable distance the road was lined in an unsightly fashion with what looked like gigantic bushes growing out of the stumps of the once tall and beautiful trees.

I have said nothing in this section as to Amiens itself; it had serious enough troubles, although it was never in the fighting zone, having been evacuated by the Germans after only ten days' occupation in September, 1914. That time, however, was sufficient for a requisition of half a million francs to be enforced, and for a number of civilians to be deported.

Some parts of the city, including the railway-station, were seriously damaged by bombing and by heavy shells, and the city suffered much from April to June in 1918. The civilian inhabitants left it early in April. Several shells hit the cathedral, and houses within a few yards of it are entirely wrecked, but happily very little damage was done to the structure itself, from which the stained glass had been safely removed.

PLATE LI.

THE SOMME ROAD.

A stretch, close to Villers Carbonnel, of the main road from Amiens towards Brie and Péronne, which lies on the high country above the Somme. What was once the avenue of trees is even here not so entirely destroyed as in many other places.

PLATE LII.

FOUCAUCOURT.

The remains of a church beside the Somme road.

PLATE LIII.

MAMETZ.

The village of Mametz has practically disappeared; the immediate foreground covers what had once been cottages; the cottages on the other side have equally disappeared. (The cross is a war memorial.)

PLATE LIV.

TRONES WOOD.

Shell-holes, chalk trenches and bare trunks are all that remain of the wood, the trunks much more numerous than in the Ypres Salient.

PLATE LV.

DELVILLE WOOD.

There is here less than in Trones Wood of chalky holes, everything is thickly covered with rank weeds, but along the roadsides even the stumps of the trees disappear after a short distance.

PLATE LVI.

COMBLES.

Remembering the amount of fighting which went on round Combles before the French and the British entered the village simultaneously from opposite sides, there are possibly more buildings left than might have been expected. They are mostly, however, even more damaged than the one which is here being examined by its owner with a view to rebuilding.

PLATE LVII.

THE BAPAUME ROAD.

The road from Albert to Bapaume by Le Sars. The chalky mound on the right is the Butte de Warlencourt, the end of the Warlencourt Ridges, which was the scene of some notably plucky fighting in November, 1916.

PLATE LVIII.

MONT ST. QUENTIN.

A bridge, not entirely destroyed by the Germans, over the dry bed of the Canal du Nord, where its course circles round the rising ground known as Mont St. Quentin, which formed so important a defence for Péronne on the north.

PLATE LIX.

PÉRONNE.

The Church of St. Jean at Péronne, according to people on the spot, was deliberately destroyed by the Germans before they were compelled finally to evacuate the town.

PLATE LX.

WARFUSÉE (LAMOTTE).

This little village church, on the Somme road, was just at the cross-roads leading to Hamel in one direction and Marcelcave in the other, both villages having some special interest both for Australians and Americans and for the Tank Corps, in the advance of August, 1918.

PLATE LXI.

VILLERS BRETONNEUX.

The village had a notable history as the vantage-point over Amiens which was the special objective of the Germans in March and April, 1918, but which they only succeeded once in holding for twenty-four hours. The Hotel of the Three Sparrows was the only one which I found in 1919.

PLATE LXII.

THE CHIPILLY SPUR.

A little salient of rising ground on the north of the Somme, filling up a bend in the river, taken by the Londoners after very hard fighting in August, 1918, with the friendly aid of a few Americans who are said to have lost their bearings, but were ready for a fight wherever they found themselves.

PLATE LXIII.

CAPPY.

One of the many destroyed villages along the Somme. The water here is only the canalised branch of the river, the rest of the stream spreads itself out to the north on the flat valley bottom.

PLATE LXIV.

VILLERS CARBONNEL.

An official photograph of the village just after we had passed it and before the débris was tidied up. The aspect of solidity about the cottages is much more apparent than real. In 1919 scarcely anything was visible which could be called a building.

PLATE LXV.

CLÉRY.

Cléry lies a little north of Péronne and below the great bend of the Somme. The photograph gives some idea of the difficulties which we had to encounter in getting an army across the river at Brie, and which the Australians had to meet, close to Cléry, in the memorable crossing on the 31st of August, 1918, after which they were able the next day to take Mont St. Quentin and enter Péronne.

PLATE LXVI.

THE CHÂTEAU OF BRIE.

At Brie the road from Amiens crosses the Somme, continuing on to the east for St. Quentin, and turning north to Péronne.

It was here that the trials were made—on the Somme—in September, 1918, of the various appliances used two days later in the audacious crossing of the deep water forming a part of the Hindenburg Line at the St. Quentin Canal, which proved so splendidly successful.

PLATE LXVII.

ON THE AMIENS-ALBERT ROAD.

At a little village (Lahoussoye), beyond Pont Noyelles on the road to Albert, stands, or stood, this dilapidated barn, carrying the scrawl written by some cheerful "Tommy"— "Pessimists shot on sight."

PLATE LXVIII.

ALBERT ON EVACUATION.

An official photograph of one of the main entries to the town just after we had regained it in August, 1918. This photograph, and also Plate LXIX, *may well be compared with Plates* LXXIX *and* LXXXVIII, *as showing the original naked devastation by contrast with the state of places after the sappers had been at work, and the inhabitants had begun to return.*

VIII.—ALBERT AND THE ANCRE

(PLATES 67 TO 73.)

HALF a dozen miles from Amiens on the road to Albert one crosses the valley of a little stream at Pont Noyelles—an untouched valley, beautiful with tall trees and green meadows like a bit of Middlesex. The road climbs the combe on the eastern bank, and a little farther on crosses the narrow space "that just divides the desert from the sown." Onwards on the high ground from this point all greenness and beauty have disappeared, every tree has gone, and at one bound is reached the "desert" which covers thousands of square miles to east and north and south. Close to the point of change it was cheering to come across the inscription (Plate 67), doubtless scrawled by some plucky "Tommy" in the bad spring days of 1918, "Pessimists shot on sight." One hopes that the cheerful artist got through safely; it was just his spirit that gave the army that final victory which they believed in as strongly in our worst hours as at any other time.

The French had compelled the Germans to leave Albert in December, 1914, and it remained in the hands of the Allies until the German advance in 1918, when it was captured on the 27th of March. It was finally retaken by us on the 22nd of August. The little industrial town, originally containing some 7,000 inhabitants, was severely shelled during years by the Germans, and then for four months by ourselves, and reduced absolutely to ruins. Plate 68 is one of those officially taken, and gives a vivid idea of the condition of one of the principal streets of approach just after we had retaken it.

In April of 1919 (Plate 69)[30] it remained a ruin, and even a year later it could hardly be otherwise described. (I believe that Plates 68 and 69 correspond to nearly the same places.) But motoring through it some nine months after the Armistice, while it was still to all appearance very much in the condition indicated by the photographs, we were practically held up about 10 o'clock in the forenoon by a stream of some hundreds of people, carrying bags and all sorts of receptacles, making their way towards the railway-station. They must no doubt have found, somewhere, shelter enough to live and sleep in in cellars or otherwise, in spite of the destruction, and were on their way to Amiens to lay in supplies.

It was on the tower of the pilgrimage Church of Notre Dame de Brebières that there stood for so long a statue of the Madonna in a position which appeared to defy gravity, and which provoked the prophecy that its fall would indicate the end of the war. The prophecy was not exactly fulfilled, but the great heap of rubbish in front of the church (Plate 70) is all that was left of the tower after our shelling of the town in 1918.

The road northwards from Albert to Miraumont (Plate 71) runs in the broad marshy valley of the River Ancre. The valley was originally thickly wooded, but was in 1918 covered with fallen tree-trunks, and Plate 72, which was taken close to Aveluy, gives some idea of its appearance. The ground on each side of the valley rises somewhat steeply for some 300 feet. The high ground on the east of the valley is that on which Thiepval and the German redoubts lay. On the west, farther north, lie Beaucourt, Beaumont-Hamel, and Miraumont, all of which were repeatedly the scenes of very heavy fighting. Beaucourt and Beaumont-Hamel were taken only at the very end of the 1916 campaign, in a short spell of possible weather.[31] Haig describes the defences here as of special and enormous strength.

At Beaumont-Hamel there was literally hand-to-hand fighting of the most severe kind. Mr. O'Neill describes the action graphically:

"On many occasions sandwiches of Scots and Germans wrestled and strove in the constricted space.... Bodies of men were prisoners and captors many times over before the struggle approached a decision.... In the midst of the fighting vast stores were tapped, and the men began to smoke as they went about their business. Some of them found time to change their underclothing when a large supply of spare shirts was found."[32]

And these men were not even the "Contemptibles," but only "mercenaries" who had been civilians till a year or so before! Truly the German preconceived notions as to the British must have suffered rude shocks.

Plate 73 (again from an official photograph) was taken after the 1918 fighting, which covered episodes as noteworthy as those of four years earlier. The photograph is taken from a point near the "cross-roads" at Beaumont-Hamel, looking across the Ancre valley to the northern (lower) end of the Thiepval Ridge, and beyond it to the higher ground on which Bapaume stands.

The final attack across the Ancre began under Thiepval, when troops of the 14th Welsh crossed the river, wading breast deep through the flooded stream under heavy fire, holding their rifles and pouches above their heads, and formed up in the actual process of a German counter-attack, along the line held by the two companies who had crossed the previous morning.[33] A day later a part of the 64th Brigade (New Zealanders) started at 11.30 p.m. on a pitch-dark night, crossed the valley, and gained and held positions, half surrounded, until the covering troops arrived. This was on the slope near Miraumont seen across the valley in Plate 73.

PLATE LXIX.

ALBERT IN WINTER.

The ruins of Albert under snow in the early spring of 1919.

PLATE LXX.

ALBERT CATHEDRAL.

The great heap of stone and brick rubbish was once the tower on which stood for a long time a statue of the Madonna at an angle which appeared to defy gravity. I am afraid that it was our shelling in 1918 which eventually brought it down.

PLATE LXXI.

IN THE ANCRE VALLEY.

The road along the Ancre Valley, entering Albert from the north.

PLATE LXXII.

AVELUY.

The swampy, but once well wooded, valley of the Ancre, with the Thiepval Ridge as its farther bank.

IX.—THE OISE AND THE AVRE

(PLATES 74 TO 78.)

IN the northern outskirts of the Forest of St. Gobain, a couple of miles from the village of Crépy, and about seven miles east of La Fère and the Oise, are to be found the remains of the emplacement (Plate 74) of the "Grosse Bertha," the gun which bombarded Paris from a distance of about seventy-four miles. On the spot we were told that there had been three guns, or at any rate three emplacements, but that the other emplacements were still more completely destroyed than the one which I have photographed. The guns and gun-carriages were, of course, removed by the Germans before we could reach them. We know, however, that the shell was about 8 inches in diameter and was fired from a large naval gun, probably similar to the gun captured at Chuignes (p. 45), lined up for the small shell. The stories that some mysterious new ballistics were involved in the matter were, of course, entirely "buncombe." But naturally the trajectory of a shell travelling more than seventy miles was a matter of interest to all artillerymen. It must have reached a height of something like five-and-twenty miles, and our knowledge of atmospheric conditions at that height is somewhat limited. The alignment of the gun, with the allowances for wind and drift, must have been very accurately calculated and carried out, for even the whole of Paris is not a large target under such exceptional circumstances.

It will not be forgotten, as a characteristic piece of German mentality—or brutality—that this gun was used on Good Friday (the 29th of March, 1918), and a shell burst in a Paris church during service and killed many of the congregation. But the Parisians, after the first shock, were to be as little scared by Bertha as the Londoners by the Zepps.

Crossing the Forest of St. Gobain—which had been continuously within the German lines—by the very worst stretches of road which I found anywhere, even in Flanders—I came across a German O.P. (Plate 75) in a tall tree. The forest itself is very fine, quite untouched by shell-fire, but the group of large, pleasant-looking country houses at St. Gobain itself have been much injured. Farther south reconstruction was in rapid progress. At the little manufacturing town of Chauny (half-way to Noyon) we found the odd condition of affairs that half the town had been entirely destroyed and the other half—the division was quite a sharp one—almost untouched.

In the early part of the war—September, 1914—when the French occupied Péronne, there was hard fighting about Noyon; at that time the Germans were too strong and the French had to fall back, but they both recovered and relost it later on. In 1917 they took Noyon once more during the great German retirement, but again it passed into German hands during the March advance in 1918, to be abandoned finally by the enemy on the 29th of August. After changing hands so often it is not to be wondered at that the town is a good deal damaged. It is not, however, totally destroyed. The cathedral (Plate 76) is a building dating from the eleventh and twelfth centuries, with very interesting architectural features. It has been greatly injured by shell-fire, roof and vaulting having mostly gone and the towers being much damaged.

Toward the end of their great advance in 1918 the Germans succeeded (on the 28th of March) in crossing the little River Doms (a southern tributary of the Avre), on which Montdidier (Plate 77) stands, and this little town, which was entirely ruined (but by this time is largely rebuilt), formed the south-western apex of their advance. Farther north, on the Avre itself, they took Moreuil and Morisel on the 29th of March, and within the next few days crossed the river and reached—from there southwards to Montdidier—the higher ground on the west of the valley, which forms the background in Plate 78. They were here, for the time, about ten miles south-east of Amiens, just as beyond Villers Bretonneux they were the same distance west. The photograph shows how exceedingly thin the coating of soil over the chalk in this district is, all the shell-holes (they are quite small) showing up like patches of snow. The little Avre River runs under the line of trees in the distance at the foot of the higher ground which the Germans had reached.

The main road southwards in the Avre valley lies here for a long distance between banks which are still riddled with German dugouts and French defences dating from the fighting of 1918.

Five days after Foch had started the great counter-offensive in July the German lines here were attacked by French troops, with some British tanks in aid, and were driven back to the Avre. The attack was in many ways a notable one, perhaps especially for the tanks, but was only a preliminary before the great advance of the 8th of August (p. 44), when at one bound the Avre was passed and the Germans pushed six miles westward.

Montdidier was surrounded by the French three days later, its garrison surrendered, and the great advance continued its inexorable progress.

PLATE LXXIII.

BEAUMONT-HAMEL.

An official photograph taken from near the cross-roads at Beaumont-Hamel looking across the Ancre Valley to the northern part of the Thiepval Ridge, towards Miraumont.

PLATE LXXIV.

THE "BIG BERTHA" EMPLACEMENT.

All that is left of an emplacement of the "Grosse Bertha," one of the guns in the St. Gobain Forest between La Fère and Laon, which shelled Paris from a distance of about seventy-four miles.

PLATE LXXV.

THE ST. GOBAIN FOREST.

The St. Gobain Forest was in German hands throughout the war; the photograph shows a German O.P. in a tall tree on high ground which would command the Oise valley in the direction of Chauny.

PLATE LXXVI.

NOYON.

The fine twelfth-century Cathedral of Noyon is even more entirely ruined, throughout much of its length, than the Cathedral of Soissons, and very much more than Rheims.

PLATE LXXVII.

MONTDIDIER.

This little town was the farthest south point reached by the Germans in their Somme advance of 1918. It lies on the Doms, which is practically a continuation of the Avre.

PLATE LXXVIII.

THE AVRE VALLEY.

The chalk here, just below Moreuil, is so near the surface that the shell-holes still looked like snow patches more than a year after they had been formed. The ground shown is that of the French counter-attack (with English tanks) a few days before the advance on the Somme in August, 1918.

PLATE LXXIX.

CAMBRAI PLACE D'ARMES.

A portion of the Place d'Armes in Cambrai, burnt deliberately by the Germans in their final evacuation, after there had been time to clear away the débris with which it had been covered.

PLATE LXXX.

CAMBRAI CATHEDRAL.

The tower of the modern Cathedral of Notre Dame at Cambrai appears to stand, in its upper part, in defiance of all theories of stable construction in masonry.

X.—CAMBRAI TO ST. QUENTIN

(PLATES 79 TO 87.)

WEST of Cambrai and south to St. Quentin lay over thirty miles of the strongest part of the Hindenburg Line, that "granite wall of 24,000 square kilometres." The southern end of the much-talked-of "Switch Line" at Quéant, ten miles west of Cambrai, had been forced by the First and Third Armies on the 2nd of September, 1918, but the defence was still strong, and it was only on the 10th of October that I was greeted, on arriving at Colonel Gill's quarters, with the welcome news that Cambrai had just fallen. Two days later I was able to visit the city. The central part (Plate 79) was still burning, having been fired by the Germans on their evacuation, but it was possible to get round by the suburbs; only an occasional shell still reached the town. (It is hardly necessary to say that the photograph, taken many months later, shows the Place d'Armes only after it had been cleared up, and not in the state in which it was when the city was entered.) The railway-station was destroyed, the windows of most houses had disappeared, and walls were cracked everywhere. But on the whole the destruction (obviously largely due to bombing as well as shell-fire) was not nearly so complete or so irreparable as at Rheims or Ypres or Lens. The tower of the cathedral (Plate 80), a church rebuilt about sixty years ago, looks as if it could hardly stand permanently. There were many houses in the suburbs which, although much damaged, could be made habitable without very serious difficulty. But it is to be remembered that the wanton destruction of household property, down to the very toys of the children, must have caused the returning inhabitants here and in many other places even more intense feeling about the invaders than the mere destruction of the houses themselves, which had come to be recognised as an inevitable consequence of the state of war, and might, in fact, have been caused by combatants on either side.

I have before me an airplane plan of Cambrai, which I obtained from the First Army in 1918 and which is an excellent example of the great skill and success we had obtained in aerial surveys. As it is printed it is very nearly a map on a scale of 6 inches to the mile, although it is a mosaic of prints from eight or nine different negatives, taken, as the direction of the shadows shows, at at least four different times. But the joins between the different prints are in many cases invisible, and the map as a whole only wants the names of the streets to make it complete.

West of Cambrai, about four miles on the road to Bapaume, and on a little rising ground, stands the Bourlon Wood, which has for us a history perhaps even more tragic than that of the woods north of the Somme. The full story of our attempt to take Cambrai in November, 1917, the first accounts of which induced foolish authorities to have "joybells" rung (a proceeding which they must have bitterly regretted afterwards), is given in Haig's Despatches (pp. 153-171). The large-scale map by which it is accompanied shows how we gained the wood, and were, in fact, close to Cambrai for a week, but a week later had lost nearly the whole of our gains. The photograph (Plate 81) is taken from the village at the north-west corner of the wood, the farthest point which we reached on the 23rd-24th November. It was in this fighting that a small party of East Surreys were rescued after having held out, surrounded, for forty-eight hours, while later on a company of the 13th Essex, entirely surrounded and without hope of relief, fought to the last man rather than surrender. Bourlon Wood was only recovered, in our final great advance, on the 27th of September, 1918.

The road from Cambrai to Le Cateau, the scene of so much fighting both in August, 1914, and in October, 1918 (see p. [78](78)), runs eastwards from Cambrai. I was able to visit a number of the villages south of the road in October, 1918 (finding in some houses the hastily left meals of their late German occupants), while fighting still continued a few miles farther north, and was surprised to find that they were very little injured in spite of the indications of heavy barrage over the face of the ground. The fighting here had gone over the ground too rapidly to leave behind it the fearful trail of destruction which is everywhere visible on the land where fighting was continuous for many weeks, or even months, together.

The south-eastern suburbs of Cambrai and the villages on that side of the town show no very extensive signs of destruction, but on the south-west and farther to the south, where the fighting across the Hindenburg Line was so severe, everything is destroyed. West of Cambrai, and for many miles to the south, lay the part of the Hindenburg defences known as the Siegfried Line, the strongest section of which, and that part deemed by the Germans to be practically impregnable, included the deep cutting of the canal between Bellicourt (Riqueval) and Bellenglise. For 6,000 yards before reaching Bellicourt the canal runs in a tunnel, the southern end of which, and the high ground above it, as well as the village of Bellicourt, is seen in Plate 82. The Americans had been told off to deal with the country over the tunnel, and did so quite successfully, but they unfortunately neglected to clear up behind them, so that the Germans, getting up from the tunnel by shafts which they had provided for the purpose, attacked them from the rear with serious consequences, and the Australians, following on, had a somewhat hard time. We had some talk with a good lady and her family who lived in a house just above the mouth of the tunnel, in which a number of German officers had been quartered. It was curious to notice how, after beginning to speak quite quietly, she and her daughter became more and more excited as their recital continued, under the recollection of the nightmare of the German occupation, although in this case there had happily been no special brutality to bring to mind.

Southwards for a couple of miles from Bellicourt towards Bellenglise the canal runs in the deep cutting seen in Plate 83, which was taken from above the tunnel mouth. The banks of the cutting are 60 or 70 feet high, very steep, and covered with thick vegetation—covered also, in 1918, with barbed wire. On the east side the bank carried, in addition, many concrete machine-gun emplacements. The water in the canal was very deep near the tunnel, and did not shallow until it nearly reached Bellenglise. The attack was carried out by Midland Territorials (Stafford and Lancashire), and had immediate success. It is specially mentioned by General Haig, and well described by General Maurice, and with natural enthusiasm and much detail by Major Priestley.[34] It was preceded by a barrage, lasting forty-eight hours, from about 1,600 guns of various calibres, and then—for once—the weather favoured us, for at zero hour, 5.50, on the morning of the attack (the 29th of September)[35] the whole country was covered with a thick fog, under which our men advanced, invisible to their enemies, although with some difficulty to themselves. The 46th Division scrambled down the cutting (where it will be seen that there was no jumping-off place on that side), and got across by swimming (with life-belts), by improvised rafts and collapsible boats, and all the devices which had been tested on the Somme at Brie (see Plate 66) a few days earlier. It seems uncertain whether any of the German foot-bridges had been left undestroyed, but the Riqueval Bridge (Plate 84) had not been knocked down by our shelling, and still stood as it was when I last saw it, carrying a notice that it was safe "for infantry in file only." Major Priestley tells the story of how Captain Charlton, with a small party of nine men, found his way by compass to the bridge, charged down on the sentries (one N.C.O. getting four of them just in time), cut the wires, and threw the blasting charges into the canal. The bridge was saved and held by 8.30, and naturally proved most useful.

Among Major Priestley's stories of this adventure he tells how two R.A.M.C. privates (Moseley and George) collected prisoners, dressed the wounded and made the prisoners carry them, and finally arrived at quarters as the sole escort of twenty stretcher cases and seventy-five unwounded prisoners.[36]

At Bellenglise (at the bend of the canal two miles south of Bellicourt) the Germans had made for themselves an extraordinary underground tunnel shelter, of which Plate 85 shows one of the entrances. We were told by the villagers that it was a kilometre and a half in length, but did not verify this. In any case it was certainly fitted up as barracks and quarters of the most extensive nature, for a thousand prisoners were taken in it with no resistance. It was also provided with electric light, and we are told that the captured electricians who were instructed to start the dynamo for us had to confess the existence of a booby-trap to blow up the whole affair when the switch was closed, and, of course, to remove it.

St. Quentin is five miles south of Bellenglise, but the crossing of the Hindenburg Line at the canal tunnel at St. Tronquoy, a necessary preliminary to taking the city, proved a task almost as difficult, but quite as successfully carried out, as the Bellicourt crossing. It was effected on the 30th of September. St. Quentin itself, which had been within the German lines ever since 1914, was entered by the French First Army on the next day. When it became clear to the Germans that they would have to give up the town, which was but little damaged, they prepared a characteristic piece of devilment, one which could not by any exercise of imagination be supposed to have the slightest military consequence. They cut out large recesses (each of about a couple of cubic feet) in the walls and columns of the cathedral, with the intention of using the cavities so made for blasting charges to wreck the whole building (Plate 86). I did not count the number of these holes, but it was officially stated to be ninety! Happily the French got into the town twenty-four hours before their entry had been expected, so that the church still stands (not, of course, without some other damage), with the holes and the blocks cut out from them visible as damning evidence of what otherwise would be no doubt denied. But very much the same seems to have been done by the same savages at other places, as far apart even as Péronne and Beersheba.

The region between the Arras-Péronne and the Cambrai-St. Quentin roads has been fought over both by French and British. Going eastwards from the crossing of the Somme at Brie the country already showed signs of renewed cultivation, but some villages, like Mons and Bernes, were totally destroyed, and others, like Estrées, Vraignes, and Hancourt, and the little town of Vermand, had been very badly strafed. Near Cambrai, villages such as Bony and Vendhuille, Gouzeaucourt and Ribécourt (Plate 87), and of course Bourlon, were quite in ruins. At Gouzeaucourt very active reconstruction was, however, going on, and rows of neat brick cottages had already appeared. To mention all the ruined villages would be to give almost a complete list of them, but over the whole region active and obviously successful attempts were being made to carry on cultivation, the surface having been by no means so badly damaged as farther north.

Southwards from St. Quentin, also, much cultivation is being actively carried on, although many of the villages, such as Liez and Essigny, are badly injured; but after La Fère is reached, and beyond the Oise, cultivation is complete, and the conditions are more or less normal as far as the Ailette and the Aisne.

North of Cambrai also, on the east of the Cambrai-Douai road, where the country was always in German occupation, and behind the Hindenburg defence lines, its condition is also normal.

PLATE LXXXI.

BOURLON WOOD.

The remains of Bourlon village, in the north-west corner of the wood, which was fought for, and taken, and lost again in the Cambrai battle of November, 1917.

PLATE LXXXII.

BELLICOURT.

The south end of the 6,000-yard tunnel on the St. Quentin Canal, seen from the western bank of the canal cutting. The village of Bellicourt lies over the tunnel mouth, and the higher ground beyond is that covered by the Americans in the advance of the 29th of September, 1918.

PLATE LXXXIII.

THE ST. QUENTIN CANAL.

The canal cutting looking down from above the tunnel mouth—an "absolutely impregnable" portion of the Hindenburg Line defences.

PLATE LXXXIV.

THE RIQUEVAL BRIDGE.

The only bridge over the St. Quentin Canal which was not destroyed by the Germans before our attack on their "impregnable" position in September, 1918. A small party of the Midland Territorials, under Captain Charlton, reached it in the fog just in time to deal with the sentries, throw the charges into the water, and so save the bridge.

PLATE LXXXV.

BELLENGLISE.

One of the entrances to the immense underground workings constructed by the Germans as a part of the Hindenburg defences at the St. Quentin Canal. The elaborate workings were finally only a trap for the thousand Germans who were secured there as prisoners.

PLATE LXXXVI.
ST. QUENTIN CATHEDRAL.

The Germans cut ninety recesses in the columns and walls of the Cathedral (two are seen in the photograph) for the purpose of placing mine charges in them and destroying the whole building when they evacuated the town. The unexpected arrival of the French frustrated this diabolical plan, but the holes and the blocks cut from them remain as witnesses.

PLATE LXXXVII.

RIBÉCOURT.

This was one of the villages which were taken in the Cambrai battle, and retained in the possession of the Allies. They are all equally destroyed, but some are already half rebuilt.

PLATE LXXXVIII.

RHEIMS.

This bit of Rheims—tidied up—is a fair example of the condition to which perhaps 10,000 out of its 14,000 houses have been reduced.

XI.—RHEIMS, THE AISNE, SOISSONS

(PLATES 88 TO 97.)

RHEIMS shares with Ypres and Verdun the glory of having successfully withstood a continuous four years' siege, and with Ypres the additional distinction of having been for a long time the central point in an extraordinarily narrow salient, surrounded by the enemy practically on three sides. It is truly an ancient storm centre, unsuccessfully besieged by the English in the fourteenth century, taken by them in the fifteenth (perhaps more by intrigue than by fighting), and held until Joan of Arc turned us out after nine years' occupation. It was entered by the Germans on the 4th of September, 1870, and again on the forty-fourth anniversary of that day in 1914. But while after 1870 they held the city for two years, in 1914 they had to evacuate it after nine days only. They commenced immediately to shell it, and, according to the universal opinion in France, to shell particularly the cathedral, in spite of official assurances that it was not used for observation purposes, which anyone but a Prussian would have believed. The north tower, unfortunately, was under repair in 1914, and covered with timber scaffolding. An incendiary shell set fire to this a week after the Germans had left the city, and the whole of the roof of the cathedral was burnt. Later on the vaulting over the transept and the choir was badly but not irreparably damaged (the statement is made that a number of Germans—the church being used as a hospital—were killed by a shell which penetrated the vaulting), and the chevet at the east end is very badly knocked about. The west end, happily, has not suffered so much, the direction of firing being generally from Brimont and Nogent l'Abesse, respectively north and east of the city. One is glad to know that it was found possible to save a certain amount of the fine stained glass.

In thinking of the fate of Rheims from the point of view of the French, it is to be remembered that to them the cathedral stands in much the same relation as does Westminster Abbey to us. It is not perhaps the finest, nor the most beautiful, nor the largest of the glorious churches of France, but it is the one which, more than any other, represents in itself and its associations the faith and the history and the life of the country over many centuries and through endless changes and vicissitudes. Considering the mentality of the Germans—as judged by the sentiments of their newspapers at the time—it may probably have been the very consciousness of the special affection of the French for the cathedral that induced them to make it their special target.

The figures which are given as to the number of shells fired, and specially the number fired at the cathedral in 1914, and on certain days in 1917, are almost unbelievable.[37]

The city has, or had before the war, about 115,000 inhabitants and some 14,000 houses. Of the latter an English visitor in 1918 informed me that about 2,000 had escaped with little damage and were more or less habitable, 2,000 more might be said to be still standing, while the remaining 10,000 were entirely destroyed. (As a comparison it may be remembered that in the Great Fire of London about 13,000 houses are said to have been burnt, or destroyed to limit the flames.)

Plate 88 is simply an example of the state of the greater part of the city, after, of course, the wreckage had been cleared off the roadways and things in general "tidied up." Plates 89 and 90 show respectively the west end of the cathedral, with its towers, and the chevet at the east end seen across a mass of ruined houses. I am afraid that the glass of the great rose windows was destroyed very early, before it could be removed, and at the east end much of the tracery of the windows has been smashed. It is in no way to the credit of the Germans, either in their intentions or in their shooting, that the damage has not been immensely greater. One may be permitted to hope that in the reconstruction of the city, which is proceeding apace, advantage will be taken of the clearance which has become unavoidable to leave such space round the building as will allow its magnificence to be more fully seen than has hitherto been possible.

After having to evacuate the city in 1914, the Germans made a very determined stand to the north at the Fort of Brimont, six miles away, as well as on the east at about the same distance, and even the desperate fighting of April, 1917, failed to move them. For the greater part of the war the French and Germans were facing each other on a north and south line a little to the east of the road from Rheims to Laon. But on their side the enemy succeeded in getting closer to the city, and the shelling must often have been at very close range, a condition of affairs more like that at Ypres than at Verdun. At one time in 1917 the Germans actually got for a day into the northern cemetery, just outside the city and only a couple of miles from the cathedral.

The remains of the French front line to the east of the Laon road were still not cleared away on my visit, the barbed-wire entanglements hardly visible above the thick growth of rank herbage. The road itself, running on a slight embankment, in places covers numerous dugouts, their entrances facing westward.

The end of September, 1918, saw the city freed at last, the Germans hastily evacuating the forts in their great retreat.

In the great retreat of the Germans in 1914 the Aisne was reached on the 12th of September, after Soissons had been in enemy occupation for ten days, during which heavy requisitions were made, although no pillage is said to have occurred. The first battle of the Aisne, the end of the German retreat in 1914, continued well into September, British artillery aiding the French north of Soissons, and Haig's troops, being farther east, attempting to reach the Chemin des Dames plateau above Troyon. But the Germans had had time to entrench themselves in the enormously strong positions afforded by the upper ground, and all the efforts of the Allies failed to dislodge them. They remained substantially unmoved until 1917, by which time they also held a sharp salient between Missy and Chavonne which had carried them across to the southern bank of the Aisne. By the beginning of 1915 the French held the valleys of Cuffies and Crouy, with the ridge between them and the western end of the high ground to the east. On the 12th-13th of January they were attacked by greatly superior numbers by Von Kluck, and, by the misfortune that floods on the Aisne had carried away their bridges higher up the stream, were cut off from their supplies, and had to retire south of the river, losing the bridge-head on the north bank. Soissons itself, however, was not captured, although the Germans remained within very easy shelling distance of it.

The Aisne winds along a flat valley bottom in great bends, always bounded on the north by high ground, which rises some 400 to 450 feet above the river, and is traversed by steep and narrow wooded ravines very much like Surrey combes, which were occupied and fully utilised by the enemy. Along the top of the plateau runs from west to east the road which became so familiar to us as the "Chemin des Dames," although this picturesque name did not appear on the maps. The main road from Soissons to Laon crosses the western end of the plateau close to the Malmaison Fort; its eastern end passes through Craonne, and the ground falls quickly down to the level of the Rheims-Laon road at Corbeny. Every foot of the "Ladies' Road" has been fought over; the whole plateau is shell-pocked almost as badly as ground beside the Amiens-Péronne road on the Somme, and the road itself is in many places no longer distinguishable, the whole area being thickly overgrown with rank herbage. Plate 91 gives some idea of what the once well-marked road now looks like where it crosses the Troyon road, the route by which Haig's troops tried in vain to reach and hold the high ground. The village of Cerny, close to the crossing, is wiped out, some hint only of its former position being indicated by the remains of what has probably been a sugar factory (Plate 92).

In many places on the slopes above the Aisne there are quarries and natural caves, greatly enlarged and very fully utilised in the German defence. Plate

93 shows one of these caves at Crouy, a now ruined village a couple of miles above Soissons on the side of the valley in which runs the little stream that descends from Laffaux on the north to the Aisne at Soissons. Beside and across this stream our artillery had hard fighting in 1914, in the vain attempt to dislodge the enemy from the high ground above and to the west, at a time when the Germans could fire twenty shells to one of ours.

The Aisne valley remained in general fairly quiescent from 1914 until April, 1917, when General Nivelle, after his great success at Verdun, planned the gigantic blow at the German front from Soissons to the Argonne, which, in spite of its ultimate success in carrying nearly the whole of the Chemin des Dames, failed to relieve Rheims,[38] and by falling so far short of the hoped-for and too optimistically predicted success helped to cause considerable, although happily only temporary, discontent in parts of the French Army, which was only cleared away by the magnificent way in which Pétain showed his men a few months later, both on the Aisne and at Verdun, that they still remained more than a match for their opponents.

The last battle of the Aisne formed the third of the series of great advances which Ludendorff had made in March and April, 1918. In each of the first two the Allies had been driven back so far and so definitely as to enable the Germans to claim overwhelming victory. But each of them, all the same, had finally found the victorious troops face to face with undefeated and immovable armies, and found them also too exhausted to press forward to gain those objectives which had constituted the real intention of each advance. The third Aisne battle was destined to have a similar conclusion. The German intentions had been well concealed, and their enormous concentration of troops had not been discovered, so that the attack which started suddenly on the 27th of May swept everybody off the ridge and down to the Aisne at once. The British 9th Corps (four divisions) were on the French right, brought there to rest after their hard fighting farther north! They held on at Craonne for a while, but were hopelessly outnumbered, and had to fall back with the rest of the troops. The Aisne and the Vesle were lost, and in three days the Germans had reached the Marne, and held ten miles of the river between Château Thierry and Dormans. Soissons fell on the 28th and Château Thierry a few days later, but the right, on which was still our 9th Corps, beside the French Fifth Army and some fine Italian troops, held back the invaders and succeeded in keeping them at a distance from Rheims and Epernay. Then followed counter-attacks, which were sometimes successful, and a month's quiescence, until on the 15th of July Ludendorff started the *Friedensturm* which was to have brought him peace—a German peace—but which ended in his utter ruin.

The Oise and Aisne Canal reaches (and crosses) the Aisne close to the foot of the road up to Troyon. The canal was no doubt dry during the war, as it was when I saw it afterwards (Plate 94), the bridge on the main road, destroyed during the German retreat, having been replaced by another.

North of the Aisne, from Soissons to Berry-au-Bac, all the villages except one appeared to be in ruins.

The whole of the country south of the Aisne to the Vesle, and again south to the Marne, was fought over in 1914, and again in the German advance in May, 1918, as well as in their final retreat in July and August. The villages, so far as I saw them, were in ruins—such, for example, as Fismes (Plate 95)—but were still recognisable as villages without the necessity, as on the Somme, of a notice-board on the roadside saying "This was ..."

Soissons itself was never far enough from the German lines to be free from shell-fire until October, 1917; it has not been, however, nearly so completely destroyed as Rheims, a reasonable number of houses remaining habitable in the end of 1918. The Germans entered it again in May, 1918, and remained in possession for two months, and during this occupation they had apparently repented of their moderation four years before, for they pillaged and stole systematically, and destroyed wantonly what they did not wish to steal.

The beautiful towers and spires of the west front of St. Jean des Vignes (Plate 96), which were all that remained of the once noble church, are a good deal damaged. It is stated that this church was pulled down in 1805 on the demand of the Bishop of Soissons in order to provide material for the repair of the cathedral, but that the two towers and spires were spared on the entreaty of the inhabitants.[39] Certainly only the skeleton of the west end with the towers has been in existence for a very long time. Apparently there have been other Huns than the Germans! The cathedral itself (Plate 97) has actually been cut in half and its one tower (the northern tower had never been built) knocked to pieces. The cathedral, although a small one, was a very beautiful structure, and was more or less unique in being arranged as two churches, one lying east and west, and the other across the transepts at right angles. The view in Plate 97 was taken in 1920 across what is now a fine open space, but which was, on my pre-war visits to the city, covered closely with houses and shops, and in 1919 was still a mass of broken walls and stone rubbish. It can be said, at any rate, that the view of the cathedral—or what is left of it—is certainly much more complete and effective than it ever had been before.

West of Soissons the destruction of villages continues for seven or eight miles along the valley, as far as Pontarchet, but still farther west, and to the south in the Compiègne forest, there are very few signs of fighting.

PLATE LXXXIX.

RHEIMS CATHEDRAL—WEST END.

The west front of the Westminster Abbey of France is happily not irreparably damaged, but the glass of the rose window has gone, and some of the statues and the carvings are injured. The roof of the building has gone entirely, and the vaulting is broken through in places.

PLATE XC.

RHEIMS CATHEDRAL—EAST END.

The east end of the Cathedral is very much more injured than the west, having been more exposed to the fire from the forts which were shelling the city.

PLATE XCI.

THE CHEMIN DES DAMES.

The road crossing the photograph from right to left is the Troyon road up from the Aisne valley. It is still practicable for motors. What is left of the Chemin des Dames itself, at this place (near Cerny), starts from the right-hand corner of the view, crosses the Troyon road, and practically disappears in the wilderness.

PLATE XCII.

THE CHEMIN DES DAMES—CERNY.

All that seemed to be left of the village of Cerny—the remains, apparently, of a sugar factory—with some water-logged shell-holes.

XII.—VERDUN, THE MEUSE, AND THE ARGONNE

(PLATES 98 TO 106.)

AFTER the first battle of the Marne, in 1914, the Germans were driven back to positions encircling Verdun on three sides (north-west, north-east, and south-east) at a distance of ten to twelve miles. They succeeded, however, in holding a little salient at St. Mihiel, on the eastern bank of the Meuse, about twenty miles south of Verdun, and with it the village of Chauvoncourt, on the west side of the river. This village was entered by the French in November, 1914, but immediately blown up (it had been already mined) by the Germans, and regained by them in a counter-attack. It remained in their hands until 1918, but they were so tightly held all round by the French that they could make no use of it as a bridge-head.

The possession of the St. Mihiel Salient, however, gave the Germans command of a stretch of the main road in the Meuse valley, and enabled them to cut the only full-gauge railway which still connected Verdun with the rest of France. This road and railway were therefore, until the successful American attack of September, 1918, entirely useless to the city, and its only railway was the narrow-gauge line leading southwards to the main line at Bar-le-Duc, and the one main road to the same place *via* Souilly. The latter came to be known as the "Sacred Way" (*La Voie Sacrée*), and became the principal line of communication for men, munitions, and stores. It is stated that thirteen battalions of infantry were occupied in keeping it in such repair as was possible, and that 1,700 lorries passed over it daily. In 1919 the northern part of the Voie Sacrée was still as bumpy for motoring as many of the worst roads in Flanders.

PLATE XCIII.

CAVES ABOVE SOISSONS.

Beside the Laon road, going northwards from Soissons, are a number of old limestone caves, partly natural and largely artificial, which were made useful by the Germans in their long occupation of this region.

PLATE XCIV.

THE OISE AND AISNE CANAL.

The dry bed of the Oise and Aisne Canal, with the original bridge blown up in the German retreat, and the French girder bridge replacing it.

PLATE XCV.

FISMES.

The townlet of Fismes, on the Vesle, like many other places between the Aisne and the Marne, has been shelled in turn by French and Germans. It is practically destroyed, but without being levelled to the ground and swallowed up by weeds like villages farther north.

PLATE XCVI.

SOISSONS—ST. JEAN DES VIGNES.

Only these two towers, with their beautiful spires, have remained of this church for more than a century. One of the towers has been so damaged as to present strange problems to an engineer in the strength of materials.

The great attack on Verdun was intended to capture the city in four days and to clear the way to Paris at one swoop, and the Emperor (whose presence never seemed to bring good fortune to his troops) was waiting at Ornes, some eight or ten miles north, to make his triumphal entry. The attack began with enormous impetuosity on the 21st of February, 1916, but in four days—with enormous losses on both sides, but chiefly to the attackers—the Germans were still held some four or five miles away from their objective on the east side of the river, and double as far on the west. But nearer the Argonne their positions had allowed them already to cut the full-gauge railway to St. Menehould by shell-fire.

A book written by General von Zwehl[40] gives the number of guns used in this attack as being about 230 in each of three corps. He also speaks of the "dejection and pessimism" induced in his troops by the failure of the artillery to make the clear way to the city which had been predicted and promised.

The Douaumont Fort was entered on the 25th, and the Emperor had sent to Berlin the news that the "key of the last defences of Verdun" was in German hands. But on the next day Pétain began counter-attacks, and although during several months the Germans made progress from time to time, eventually gaining the Vaux Fort and most of the Mort Homme Ridge, the great attack had, in reality, miscarried from the start.

The city itself, from which all civilians had been evacuated by the 25th of February, was heavily shelled, especially at the commencement of the attack, but as a city it has not suffered to anything like the same extent as Rheims, to say nothing of Albert, Lens, or Ypres. The fighting and the tremendous shelling were always in a zone lying roughly between four and eight miles from the city; within this zone the ground is as completely shell-marked, the villages and woods as completely destroyed, as even on the Somme.

The greatest German advance was reached in June, 1916, Thiaumont Fort being taken on the 30th of June, when at one point the Germans were only three miles from the city. Thiaumont was retaken when the French offensive started in the following October, and on the 2nd of November Vaux Fort was recovered and the Germans had been driven back nearly to the lines they had succeeded in occupying on the 24th of February. But the Mort Homme Ridge was entirely regained only in August, 1917, and it was still another year before it could be said that Verdun was entirely "cleared." The final success of the French in driving back the enemy is attributed by General von Zwehl to the overwhelming superiority of their artillery, the German heavy guns having been sent elsewhere.

Plate 98, taken from the left bank of the Meuse, shows the broken bridge at St. Mihiel and the ridge above; the little town lies chiefly beyond the picture in a hollow on the right. It has been very little damaged; even the great clock in the church tower is uninjured. It is easily seen how entirely the ridge, some 300 feet above the river and filling up an acute bend, enabled the Germans to dominate the road and railway on the left bank for a long distance. In April, 1915, a French attack on the north side of the salient took Les Éparges after severe fighting, but made no further progress. The neighbouring country to the west of the Meuse is quite unharmed until one comes within a few miles of the river. The St. Mihiel Salient was attacked from the south by the Americans and by the French from the north on the 11th of September, 1918, just as the Germans had determined to evacuate it, and it was finally cleared within a week.

The view from the Pont Ste. Croix at Verdun over the Meuse (Plate 99) shows a portion of the most destroyed area of the city, in which some sort of reconstruction had already started. On the opposite side of the river, however, tall buildings were standing quite uninjured, and entering the city from the south by the Porte St. Victor one traverses a long length of street without seeing any serious destruction. The cathedral (not a very interesting building after many reconstructions) has been badly damaged as to its vaulting and roof, but the towers still stand; the Church of St. Saviour has been less fortunate.

PLATE XCVII.

SOISSONS CATHEDRAL.

The Cathedral of Soissons, which is so badly damaged that its reconstruction appears almost hopeless, is one of the oldest, and architecturally one of the most interesting, of the French Gothic churches.

PLATE XCVIII.

ST. MIHIEL.

The little salient of St. Mihiel, on the Meuse, twenty miles above Verdun, was secured by the Germans very early in the war, and gave them command of the principal road and railway from Verdun. It was held by them until the very end, when Americans and French together squeezed them out.

PLATE XCIX.

VERDUN.

A part of the centre of Verdun, on the Meuse. Oddly enough, buildings just opposite these, on the other side of the river, are almost untouched. But the fighting at Verdun— with which only the fighting on the Somme and in Flanders are comparable—was concentrated on the hilly ground some miles north of the city.

PLATE C.

VAUX FORT—NORTH FOSSE.

The holding of the fort at Vaux, one of those nearest Verdun, by Major Raynal and his men, was one of the finest episodes of the war. The Germans were held at bay for three months, but eventually the defenders were driven down to the underground passages connected to the North Fosse, and were overpowered after seven days' continuous fighting.

Vaux Fort—although we did not hear so much of it in England as of Douaumont—was the scene of one of the most gallant episodes of the war. The fort is somewhat less than five miles north-east of the city; it was completed only in 1911, and is a huge mass of masonry and reinforced concrete, with many underground works, on an eminence which dominates the country on the side away from the city and faces the Douaumont Ridge across a valley in which lies the village of Vaux. The tops of both Vaux and Douaumont Forts look like a wilderness of shell-holes in a gravel bed; apparently the concrete has been covered over with many feet of something in the nature of gravel as an additional protection. Vaux Fort was held against three months of incessant attacks by Major Raynal and his men, the last of whom were finally completely imprisoned within it, but held out and fought hand to hand in the steep underground passages leading to the northern fosse (Plate 100), the only outlet remaining to them. Great efforts were made to relieve them, but without success, and after a final week of continuous fighting, during the last two days of which they had only water enough for the wounded men, the little garrison was overpowered on the 8th of June, 1916. The Germans had the courtesy, in recognition of his splendid defence, to allow Major Raynal to retain his sword. The fort was finally regained on the 2nd of November of the same year.

The village of Vaux, which lies in the valley north of the fort, was fought for strenuously and eventually taken long before the fort itself. I tried to find some sign of its existence; its site is certainly somewhere in the centre of Plate 101, but such remains as may exist are entirely blotted out by the growth of the rank herbage which fills the whole valley from side to side.

The fort of Douaumont (Plate 102) was that of which the name was most familiar in this country, owing to its partial capture in the early attack and also to the absurd boasting of the Emperor, already alluded to, in connection with it. It lies to the north-west of Vaux, upon a parallel ridge. The fort was taken on the 25th of February, the fifth day of the great attack in which the French troops had been fighting continuously against "five times their strength in men and ten times their strength in guns." The Kaiser was at Ornes, waiting for its fall; men's lives were to form no hindrance to the attack; the Brandenburgers[41] succeeded in getting into it, and a few of them held on in the ruins, with the French on both sides of them. But Pétain had arrived, and the Germans were beaten, although at that time neither side knew it, and although thousands of lives had still to be sacrificed before the end arrived.

In the following May the French retook the fort, but were driven out after two days by an overwhelming attack. In October, 1916, it passed finally to the French under General Mangin, after a heavy bombardment. The troops for this attack had been trained on a complete model, constructed behind the lines, of the ground and of the fort, to familiarise them exactly with the position to be dealt with.

The earlier Verdun attacks were made upon the east side of the river, but after these were fought to a standstill fighting shifted to the western side, where it eventually reached an even greater intensity than before. The Mort Homme Ridge (Plate 103), about eight miles north-west of Verdun, lies about two miles in front of the original German positions of the 21st of February, and its possession was essential to the Germans if they were to be any more successful in reaching Verdun from the north-west than they had been from the north-east. Its highest point is about 300 feet above the city. The artillery attack commenced on the 2nd of March, and the advance four days later, but the progress made was very slow, and although the slaughter was absolutely terrific, when the fighting died down on the 9th of April—forty-eight days after it had started—the Mort Homme was still untaken.

Onwards from this date the fighting at Verdun was—at least, in comparison with what had gone before—only desultory. In May the highest point ("304") on the ridge had to be abandoned, and by the 21st of May the Germans had gained the north-east slopes of the Mort Homme. But the battle as a whole had been lost long before this, and no local gains could change its result. [Plate 103](#) shows the monument put up by the French on the southern slope of the Mort Homme to which they had been driven, a little below point 295. It is very difficult in a photograph taken from ground-level to give any idea of the surface of shell-holed ground, but something of it can be seen in this view and something also in [Plate 104](#), which shows the last French front-line positions near the top of the southern slope of the ridge, where the final attack occurred on the 28th of May, 1916. But the French front still remained unbroken; they had never even been pushed back to their main positions of defence. The great counter-attack on the left of the Meuse came in August, 1917, when the Mort Homme and Cumières Wood were retaken on the first day, and the whole original front restored in a week.

The Argonne Forest, in which the Americans had such stiff fighting in pushing back the Germans in 1918, lies about twenty miles west of Verdun and covers an area of some 150 square miles up to the line where the Aire River cuts across it on its way to the Aisne. Its huge dimensions, and the fact that only a portion of it was the scene of actual fighting for any considerable time, have saved it from undergoing the total destruction of so many of the smaller woods. [Plate 105](#) shows some of the southern portion between St. Menehould and Clermont, which is practically uninjured, although the village of Les Islettes (faintly seen in the valley, which here separates the forest into two sections) is in ruins. Along the road from St. Menehould to Verdun through the forest (from which the view was taken) there were in 1919 long lines of fruit-trees quite uninjured, an unusually cheerful sight. In September, 1914, after the first battle of the Marne, the Germans in their retreat held the northern part of the forest, practically on the cross-road from Varennes to Vienne-le-Château. From that time until the end of 1915 there was continuous and very severe fighting in the section of the forest between that road and the St. Menehould road. Fighting in the depths of the forest among thick trees, on wet and slippery ground traversed by endless ravines, was incessant by day and night, often hand to hand, and below ground as well as on the surface. The French did not succeed in dislodging the enemy, but they were successful in defeating two powerful attacks by the Crown Prince, in June and July, 1915, directed at the St. Menehould-Verdun road. The enemy got within five or six miles of Les Islettes, and the little town was destroyed, but they never got to the road, and were promptly driven back to their old lines. The town of Clermont, farther east on this road, had been sacked and then burnt by the Germans in their retreat in 1914.

Varennes (Plate 106) is on the eastern edge of the forest, where it is crossed by the River Aire, which up to that point had been flowing northwards east of the Argonne, as the Aisne does on the west. It was the headquarters of the Crown Prince's army in 1915, and his attacks in that year started from it. It is only a few miles west of Avocourt and Malancourt, from which started the March attack on the Mort Homme Ridge from the west in 1916.

After the end of 1915 the Argonne quieted down, but trench fighting and mining was always going on until the commencement of the Franco-American offensive on the 26th of September, 1918, following the American success at St. Mihiel. Among other forms of defence the Germans here used steel-wire net-screens, 3 metres high, fixed to the tree-trunks. The Americans had very hard work in getting through the forest—how severe may be judged from the fact that there are over 25,000 graves in the great American cemetery near Montfaucon; but eventually the Germans were compelled to retreat, and on the 9th of October the French from the west and the Americans from the east met at Grandpré, at the northern extremity of the forest.

PLATE CI.

VAUX VILLAGE.

The village lies in a hollow below the fort; its site is somewhere close to the place from which the photograph was taken. But all signs of the buildings—which were reduced to fragments early in the siege—have absolutely disappeared.

PLATE CII.

DOUAUMONT FORT.

The fort of Douaumont was entered, but not held, very early in the Verdun battle, and the Kaiser telegraphed to Berlin the capture of the "key to Verdun." But the lock would not open, Verdun was not taken, and the Kaiser left it to prophesy elsewhere with equal want of success.

PLATE CIII.

THE MORT HOMME.

The photograph gives only a faint idea of the shell-marked ridge whose name became so familiar to us in the Verdun campaign. Eventually a considerable part of it was taken, but the gain was useless—Verdun was as far off as ever.

PLATE CIV.

THE MORT HOMME.

The French front lines on the southern slope of the Mort Homme Ridge. From these ridges the view in all directions seems to cover nothing but shell-pocked wastes, the grave of 400,000 Frenchmen and probably of very many more Germans.

PLATE CV.

THE ARGONNE FOREST.

This southern part of the forest, on the road from St. Menehould to Verdun, has not been fought over, so that the trees are still in their natural condition. In the central valley, seen over the trees, lies Les Islettes in ruins. It was the farthest point of one of the Crown Prince's fruitless attempts to get south in 1915.

PLATE CVI.

VARENNES.

Vavenues, on the margin of the Argonne Forest, and now in ruins, was the Crown Prince's headquarters during a considerable period, when there was every day fierce fighting with the French, of which at the time we heard very little in this country.

Varennes itself (the little town where Louis XVI. was arrested in 1791 on his attempted flight from France) is very nearly destroyed. The Americans took it on the first day of their advance, when it was defended by a division of Prussian Guards, and on the next day they captured Montfaucon, the headquarters of the Crown Prince for his Verdun attack. The ground here is high, and the Germans had built themselves an excellent O.P. from the materials of the church. Here also, according to General Maurice, the Crown Prince had directed operations from a "palatial dugout."

Traces of the American occupation of this district were still visible months afterwards in the shape of road notices, "Do your bit! Obey the traffic regulations!" and it was in the familiar accent of a young American officer that we received instructions as to getting our car through the narrow streets of Verdun.

XIII—THE MARNE TO MONS

(PLATES 107 TO 124.)

ON a bright and quiet Sunday morning, the 23rd of August, 1914, General Smith-Dorrien's men were aligned along the Mons-Condé Canal (Plate 107), west of the town, on the northern edge of a thickly populated industrial district, with the great spoil heaps of the mines (Plate 108) like a range of miniature extinct volcanoes lying behind them. They had only just arrived from home, and with the failure of "Intelligence," of which they knew nothing, they were entirely ignorant of the strength and movements of their opponents. The Sabbatic quietude was broken with startling suddenness soon after noon, and very shortly the unexpected action became general along the whole front. The Germans outnumbered us by two to one both in guns and men; they were fresh from their successful outrages in overrunning Belgium, and they were full of contempt for the British "mercenaries." Their advance was excellently well covered by the terrain until they were within fairly short range, and they advanced wave on wave in close formation. They were decimated again and again by our rifle-fire, but again and again advanced in spite of it. Our men were sick of the slaughter, and their fire was so deadly that the German writers have afterwards attributed it to the enormous number of machine-guns which we were using, although we were in fact all too short, at that time, of this particular arm. The defence held out for six hours in face of the overwhelming odds, but at night we were compelled to retire, Mons itself having been entered by the enemy. So commenced the Mons retreat, so far as our men were concerned. The French retreat, unfortunately, their men being equally outnumbered, had commenced twelve hours before. On the next two days the retreat continued, Smith-Dorrien's army on the west of the Mormal Forest towards Le Cateau, and Haig's on the east of the forest towards Landrecies. The great Mormal Forest itself (some ten miles long and from three to five miles wide) has been very much thinned during the war by the Germans for the sake of its timber (Plate 109). Even now, although traversed by many woodland roads, it would be an impossible undertaking to take through it a great army in retreat, and this made the separation of the two armies unavoidable. On the 25th of August Haig's men had reached the old fortified town of Landrecies, on the Sambre. Fifty years or so before this, R. L. Stevenson—boating down the river on his "Inland Voyage"—had passed through the old-world fortifications, and wrote of the town, singularly enough:

"It was just the place to hear the round going by at night in the darkness, with the solid troop of men marching, and the startling reverberation of the drum. It reminded you that even this place was a point in the great warfaring system of Europe, and might on some future day be ringed about with cannon smoke and thunder, and make itself a name among strong towns."[42]

Hardly a "strong town" in these days, but certainly it made itself a name both at the beginning and the end of the war. At 10 o'clock on the night of the 25th of August an alarm was given; the Germans had made their way through wood roads, and tried to rush us in the camouflage of French uniforms and French words of command. Happily the 4th Guards Brigade was on the spot, although only just arrived, and received the enemy in unexpected fashion, so that by midnight the attack had collapsed, and a little more much-needed breathing-time was gained. A Landrecien told us, in 1919, how he had seen the Germans coming down "in their thousands," and how the Guards had stood up to them at the railway and road corner at which my photograph (Plate 110) was taken. In 1918 the tables were turned, and it was the German Guards who were trying to hold up our infantry, who captured the town on the 10th of October, after crossing the Sambre on rafts. It is of this attack that the story[43] is told of three *tractor* tanks, which made a bluff at a moment when the infantry were held up, and of which two got through and successfully made a way for the rifles.

South-west of the forest lies Le Cateau (Plate 111), at one end of the straight fifteen-mile road to Cambrai, south of which lie the villages of Caudry, Esnes, Ligny, and many others whose names we heard first in August, 1914, and again four years later. It was here that General Smith-Dorrien made the great stand of the 26th of August, which has been the subject of so much discussion, but which certainly gave the opportunity for most gallant fighting, both of infantry and artillery, while it held back—and, better still, greatly exhausted—the enemy. By the afternoon the position became untenable, and then followed the all-night march of the tired men towards St. Quentin. Le Cateau itself appears to be very little damaged.

On the "Roman road," running south from Le Cateau to the Cambrai-St. Quentin road, the villages are now much damaged, probably rather in 1918 than in 1914, and notices were still standing—"Do not halt on this road"— at places towards the south. Another souvenir of 1918 was a notice near Maurois, "Pip Squeaks 6.30 to-night!" A less agreeable reminiscence was a sugar factory, thoroughly gutted by the Germans in characteristic fashion, beside the road near Estrées, a village itself in ruins. Along this road, as in many places on the Somme, the route, now destitute of trees, is marked by short wooden posts on each side placed at short distances apart, their object being, of course, to keep lorries on the track in the dark, or at least to give them notice if they strayed from it. Here and there many of the posts on one side of the road seemed to be sloping in one direction, and those on the other side in the opposite direction. The obvious inference was that the slope of the posts was due to the frequency with which the lorries had run into them!

The Le Cateau battlefield was so quickly crossed both in 1914 and 1918 that many of its villages, some of which I had the opportunity of visiting while fighting was going on only a few miles farther north, are very little damaged, and the land surface generally is almost uninjured in comparison with its condition both farther north and farther south.

The 1st of September was the anniversary of Sedan, and the Germans had apparently hoped to celebrate the day in Paris. But on or about that day, perhaps the day before, Von Kluck had made the great turn to the southeast, which (whatever its original motive) eventually allowed the French to get on his flank across the Ourcq, and paved the way for the great victory on the Marne.

The Germans had progressed so far as to cross the Marne by the 4th of September, and had reached their farthest south position on the Petit Morin, which joins the Marne at La Ferté-sous-Jouarre. On the next day Joffre gave his orders for the commencement of the advance on the 6th, which at one blow turned the much-vaunted advance into a retreat, and postponed for ever the triumphal march of the Emperor through the Arc de Triomphe which was found to have been so elaborately arranged for. The bridge over the Marne at La Ferté-sous-Jouarre—close to which the photograph in [Plate 112](#) was taken—was blown up, and we failed to cross the river until two days later, after which came the great and complex battle which ended with the Germans back to the Aisne. But they still succeeded in holding, and were still to hold for four more years, all the hilly country between Rheims and Verdun, as well as Laon, St. Quentin, Péronne, and Cambrai, and also, for much of that time, the whole Somme region.

And so the war went on, until in May of 1918 Ludendorff played his last shot and swept down across the Aisne and the Vesle and the Tardenois country to the Marne once more,[44] and finally, in the *Friedensturm* (for the opening of which the Emperor came down specially on the 15th of July), crossed the river between Château Thierry (which is badly damaged), Dormans ([Plate 113](#)), and Montvoisin, and for a few days held a precarious and unhappy[45] footing on the south bank, his pontoon bridges being exposed to continual enfilade firing, and his communications only kept up very imperfectly in consequence. The ruin of the villages along the river here shows how hard the shelling had been at this time.

At length came the day when Foch could let his armies off the leash. No one can forget the thrill of that 18th of July, when the news came through in the early afternoon in the clubs and the newspapers that the advance for which we had hoped so long—and which we somehow knew with a singular certainty that Foch would make in his own time—had actually commenced. Some of us, whether more sanguine or more wise than others I cannot say, seemed to understand at once that the end had really begun, and the horrible black clouds of four years were broken up as suddenly and finally as when the sun bursts out after a thunderstorm, and the storm which was overhead a moment before is suddenly seen to be rolling away to the horizon. And when the late news at night and the early news the next morning allowed us to see something of Foch's intention, and how well things were progressing, we might well have ordered "joybells" if it had not been for our painful recollection of too early rejoicing over the Cambrai battle of 1917. But the joybells were within everyone, all the same. No doubt there is justification for the special celebration every year of Armistice Day. But to many of us the real day of relief, the day when the sun once more broke out on France and Britain and all the Allied lands, was the day on which Mangin astonished the Germans by suddenly walking through the western boundary of the salient which they had captured with so much effort and so much boastfulness.

The scheme of the *Friedensturm* was to encircle Rheims by simultaneous advances east and west of the impassable Montagne de Reims, the advances to meet at Epernay ([Plate 114](#)), and thereafter the valley of the Marne to provide the long-deferred route to Paris. On the east the advance was held up on the Vesle from the very start by General Gouraud's skilful "false front" tactics. Prunay was taken and retaken, and attempts made to secure a bridgehead at Sillery ([Plate 115](#)), six miles from the city, and due south of the Nogent de l'Abesse fort, while slight gains were made farther east; but practically no progress at all was effected.

South of Rheims and away to the south and east from Epernay towards Bar-le-Duc, the war-struck ground ceases. Pleasant avenues and undamaged villages are delightful to the eye after days of wandering in the desert of the north-west. In places we even passed through avenues of fruit-trees in full blossom.

Having failed in the east, Ludendorff redoubled his pressure on the west of the Montagne, but British troops and Italian Alpini joined the French in holding up the critical points; and although the salient round Rheims itself was narrowed, the Marne was not reached and Epernay could only be shelled from a distance of seven or eight miles. Near Château Thierry, at the western end of the great salient, American troops aided the French in preventing advance. Already on the 18th of July, the first day of the advance, the French reached positions commanding the road and railway at Soissons, on the 21st Château Thierry was recaptured, and the next day saw the Germans back, for the last time, north of the river which had been the turning-point in 1914. The 26th of July saw an engagement which earned very special appreciation from Haig,[46] the taking of the Buzancy Château (Plate 116) and the little plateau on which it stands, about 300 feet above the River Crise, some four miles south of Soissons. Buzancy had been the object of an attack by the French and another by the Americans within a week from the commencement of the advance, but had been pertinaciously held by the Germans. It is in effect a narrow promontory between two deep valleys, and an almost unassailable position. On the 28th of July the 15th Scottish Division were told off for the attack, and the Highlanders succeeded after a fight so notable that, although the position was not permanently held until a day or two later, the 17th French Division erected a memorial (Plate 117) in commemoration of it on the spot where the body of the foremost Highlander was found. The monument, simple and dignified, bears the inscription: "Ici fleurira toujours le glorieux Chardon d'Écosse parmi les Roses de France." Five days later the French entered Soissons once more, and on the 5th of August the Aisne was again crossed, and Fismes (Plate 95), on the Vesle, was taken by the Americans on the same day. But Foch's plan led him to leave this district for a time while equally important advances were made elsewhere.

On the 10th of October the troops were back again on the old Le Cateau battlefield, and Le Cateau was retaken, and on the next day the whole length of the Chemin des Dames plateau was again in the Allies' possession.

On the 4th of November we were again at Landrecies,[47] and right through the Mormal Forest, while on the next day the ancient fortifications of Le Quesnoy (Plate 118) were taken by assault and the garrison surrendered.

Meantime French and Americans were advancing farther to the east, outside the lines of the 1914 retreat, through extremely difficult country, and meeting with strenuous opposition. Near Varennes one saw still in 1920 the American notice, "Road under control; split your convoy" (see p. 75).

The Germans, retreating, naturally cut down all the trees on the roadsides in order to lay them across the roads to hinder our advance; there now remain only stumps a few feet above the ground. It must be long before the old avenues can reappear, but cultivation seemed to be going on normally everywhere. The destruction of fruit-trees in the German retreat of 1917 was a different matter, the justification of which on military grounds seems somewhat strained. Plate 119 is copied from a photograph in a captured German Report from the Hirson district. It was intended specially to show the blowing up of a railway-bridge at Mennessis, but serves also to show exactly the thorough and deliberate way in which the orchards were destroyed.

At cross-roads mine craters formed a serious delay to traffic, and the sappers (after careful investigation for, and destruction of, the numerous booby-traps) had to bridge or to circumvent them, or both. Bridges, of course, were all blown up. Hirson, entered on the 8th of November (Plate 120), is an example of many others, where there has not been time to erect a girder bridge. Plate 121 shows one of the pile bridges over the Condé Canal—bridges which were often erected in an incredibly short time. The Americans reached the Meuse at Sedan (Plate 122) on the 5th of November, and took the western half of the town on the 7th, and the British under Byng retook the ancient fortress of Maubeuge (Plate 123 shows the girder bridge over the Meuse here put across after the German retreat), which had been compelled to surrender, after a fortnight's siege, on the 9th of November in 1914. Finally British troops (Canadians) reached Mons (Plate 124), and entered the city at dawn on the 11th of November, a few hours before the Armistice came into effect. So ended the campaign where it had been commenced more than four years earlier. A story told by Mr. Buchan[48] is well worth repeating: The 8th Division in Horne's First Army had spent the winter of 1917-18 in the Ypres Salient; it had done gloriously in March in the retreat from St. Quentin; it had fought in May in the third battle of the Aisne, and from the beginning of August had been hotly engaged in the British advance:

"Yet now it had the vigour of the first month of war. On the 10th of November one of its battalions, the 2nd Middlesex, travelled for seven hours in 'buses, and then marched twenty-seven miles pushing the enemy before them. They wanted to reach the spot near Mons where some of them (then in the 4th Middlesex) fired almost the first British shots in the war, and it is pleasant to record that they succeeded."

With the recollection of this exploit and the story of Cambrai and Bourlon (and many others) before them, will anyone in future be daring enough to try to convince us of the physical and moral decadence of the Cockney—a doctrine which some offensively superior people tried to preach not so many years ago?

PLATE CVII.

THE MONS-CONDÉ CANAL.

General Smith-Dorrien's men were in position along the canal when they first received the German attack on Sunday, the 23rd of August, 1914.

PLATE CVIII.

SLAG HEAPS AT MONS.

The colliery slag heaps close to Mons, among which fighting took place on the first day of the retreat from Mons in 1914.

PLATE CIX.

THE MORMAL FOREST.

The western end of the road across the Mormal Forest to Jolimetz. The wood has been much thinned by the Germans during their four years of possession.

PLATE CX.

LANDRECIES.

Here the Guards first came into action in August, 1914, and here in 1918 the German Guards failed to stand in their retreat against our infantry.

PLATE CXI.

LE CATEAU.

The town is very little, if at all, damaged. It stands close to the "Roman Road" at the eastern end of the road to Cambrai, across and to the south of which we fought heavy rear-guard actions in 1914, and across which, in the opposite direction, the Germans retreated four years later.

PLATE CXII.

THE MARNE.

This view gives some idea of the size of the river. It was taken near La Ferté-sous-Jouarre, which was in the British lines in the first battle of the Marne in September, 1914.

PLATE CXIII.

DORMANS.

On the Marne, a few miles east of Château Thierry. It is one of the places covered in Ludendorff's Friedensturm *advance, and therefore one of those first to be recovered by Foch in 1918.*

PLATE CXIV.

EPERNAY.

Ludendorff's great attempt at encircling Rheims involved that two advances, one east and one west of the Montagne de Reims, should meet at Epernay, and thence advance on Paris by the Marne Valley. But Epernay was never reached from either side, although it was shelled from a distance of seven or eight miles.

PLATE CXV.

THE VESLE AT SILLERY.

About six miles from Rheims, where General Gouraud held up the eastern arm of Ludendorff's "pincers."

PLATE CXVI.

BUZANCY CHÂTEAU.

At the top of a little ridge above the Crise, south of Soissons. It was stormed by the Highlanders in very notable fashion in July, 1918. The plateau beyond it gave General Mangin command of the German communications farther east.

PLATE CXVII.

MONUMENT AT BUZANCY.

This memorial was erected by the 17th French Division, who took over from the Camerons, with the inscription "Ici fleurira toujours le glorieux Chardon d'Écosse parmi les Roses de France."

PLATE CXVIII.

LE QUESNOY.

An old town with Vauban fortifications, of which the photograph shows the moat, which was taken by storm in November, 1918.

PLATE CXIX.

DESTRUCTION OF ORCHARDS (1917).

A copy from a captured German photograph of a blown-up railway bridge, incidentally showing the deliberate destruction of the fruit-trees in the German retreat of 1917.

PLATE CXX.

HIRSON.

Everywhere in their retreat of 1918 the Germans naturally blew up bridges in order to hinder our progress behind them. At Hirson the old bridge was still only replaced by a timber structure.

PLATE CXXI.
A PILE BRIDGE.

One of the very rapidly constructed pile bridges (in this case over the Condé Canal), which the Engineers threw up in place of those destroyed in the German retreat.

PLATE CXXII.

SEDAN.

The River Meuse at Sedan,—where the entrance of Americans and French in 1918 avenged the catastrophe of half a century earlier.

PLATE CXXIII.

MAUBEUGE.

The fortifications of Maubeuge, although of an old type, held a considerable force of Germans back in the advance of 1914. The bridge was, of course, destroyed by the retreating Germans in 1918, and the girder bridge has temporarily replaced it.

PLATE CXXIV.

MONS.

For us the war began here on the 23rd of August, 1914, and ended on the 11th of November, 1918.

FOOTNOTES:

1. [1] Domelier, "Behind the Scenes at German Headquarters."

2. [2] Maurice, "The Last Four Months," p. 158.

3. [3] See Lord Milner's account in the *New Statesman* of the 23rd of April, 1921.

4. [4] Buchan, "History of the War," vol. xxiv., p. 78.

5. [5] Dubois, "Deux Ans de Commandement."

6. [6] Buchan, vol. vii., p. 37.

7. [7] "Journal d'une Sœur d'Ypres, October, 1914, to May, 1915."

8. [8] Probably thick wet blankets intended to be dropped when there was danger of gas.

9. [9] Bates, "Touring in 1600," p. 287.

10. [10] Haig's Despatches, vol. i., p. 133.

11. [11] See the photograph on p. 30 of the "Michelin Guide to Ypres."

12. [12] Figures in the distance are German prisoners, of whom there were a great many at the time, occupied in "clearing" operations.

13. [13] Despatches, p. 118.

14. [14] Buchan, vol. x., p. 106.

15. [15] See p. 25.

16. [16] Despatches, p. 225.

17. [17] This photograph is from a negative taken by Colonel Gill.

18. [18] Despatches, p. 226.

19. [19] Buchan, vol. x., p. 174.

20. [20] Not to be confused with the Bailleul near Armentières, or the Givenchy north of the La Bassée Canal, which were much more notable places in the war.

21. [21] Despatches, p. 101.

22. [22] O'Neill, "History of the War," p. 604.

23. [23] Haig's Despatches, p. 29.

24. [24] This view is taken looking eastwards towards Bapaume, with the Butte on the south side of the road.

25. [25] Despatches, p. 47.

26. [26] Haig's Despatches, p. 205.

27. [27] See Haig's Despatches, p. 259.

28. [28] Sir Arthur Conan Doyle, vol. vi., p. 30.

29. [29] Haig's Despatches, p. 270.

30. [30] From a negative taken by Mr. Basil Mott.

31. [31] Haig's Despatches, p. 50.

32. [32] O'Neill, "History of the War," p. 664.

33. [33] Haig's Despatches, p. 268.

34. [34] Haig's Despatches, p. 282, "The Last Four Months," p. 161, and "Crossing the Hindenburg Line," p. 48.

35. [35] We now know that it was on the 28th of September that Ludendorff met the Kaiser and insisted on the necessity for an armistice.

36. [36] Priestley, *op. cit.*, p. 63.

37. [37] Buchan's "History of the War," vol. iii., p. 71, and the "Michelin Guide to Rheims," p. 20, etc.

38. [38] Captain Tuohy in "The Secret Corps" says that the trial of a spy known as "Suzette" showed that her machinations played no small part in preventing Nivelle's success. She is alleged especially to have given the enemy full details as to the new French tanks, and also full information where and how it was intended to use them.

39. [39] "Michelin Guide to Soissons," p. 44.

40. [40] Reviewed in *The Times* Literary Supplement of the 7th of April, 1921.

41. [41] They are said to have worn French Zouave uniforms.

42. [42] "Inland Voyage," p. 69.

43. [43] Major Williams Ellis, "The Tank Corps," p. 268.

44. [44] See p. 66.

45. [45] An intercepted pigeon message from a German officer is said to have described the situation south of the river as "worse than hell."

46. [46] Haig's Despatches, vol. ii., p. 256.
47. [47] See p. 77, *ante.*
48. [48] "History of the War," xxiv., p. 73.